State Mental Hospitals and the Elderly

A Task Force Report of the American Psychiatric Association

The American Psychiatric Association Task Force on Geriatric Psychiatry in the Public Mental Health Sector

Barry S. Fogel, M.D. (Chair)
Christopher Colenda, M.D.
John M. deFigueiredo, M.D.
David Larson, M.D.
Daniel Luchins, M.D.
Gary Moak, M.D.
Josie Olympia, M.D.
Eric Pfeiffer, M.D.
Howard Waxman, Ph.D.

State Mental Hospitals and the Elderly

A Task Force Report of the American Psychiatric Association

Published by the American Psychiatric Association
Washington, DC

Note: The authors have worked to ensure that all information in this book concerning drug dosages, schedules, and routes of administration is accurate as of the time of publication and consistent with standards set by the U.S. Food and Drug Administration and the general medical community. As medical research and practice advance, however, therapeutic standards may change. For this reason and because human and mechanical errors sometimes occur, we recommend that readers follow the advice of a physician who is directly involved in their care or the care of a member of their family.

The findings, opinions, and conclusions of this report do not necessarily represent the views of the officers, trustees, all members of the task force, or all members of the American Psychiatric Association. The views expressed are those of the authors of the individual chapters. Task force reports are considered a substantive contribution of the ongoing analysis and evaluation of problems, programs, issues, and practices in a given area of concern.

Copyright © 1993 American Psychiatric Association
ALL RIGHTS RESERVED
Manufactured in the United States of America on acid-free paper
First Edition
96 95 94 93   4 3 2 1
American Psychiatric Association
1400 K Street, N.W., Washington, DC   20005

Library of Congress Cataloging-in-Publication Data
American Psychiatric Association.   Task Force on Geriatric Psychiatry
   in the Public Mental Health Sector.
      State mental hospitals and the elderly : Task Force on Geriatric
   Psychiatry in the Public Health Sector. — 1st ed.
         p.   cm.
      Includes bibliographical references and index.
      ISBN 0-89042-242-7 (alk. paper)
      1. Mentally ill aged—Institutional care—United States.   2. State
   hospitals—Government policy—United States.   3. Mental health
   policy—United States.   I. Title.
      [DNLM: 1. Hospitals, State—United States.   2. Mental Health
   Services—in old age—United States.   3. Hospitals, Psychiatric-
   -United States.   WM 30 A52555s 1993]
   RC451.4.A5A5   1993a
   362.2'1'0846—dc20
   DNLM/DLC
   for Library of Congress   93-6585
                                                                CIP

British Library Cataloguing in Publication Data
A CIP record is available from the British Library.

Contents

Acknowledgments

The Task Force acknowledges the thoughtful comments of numerous readers and consultants. These include Carl Cohen, Frank Jones, Gary Kennedy, Roger Peele, and Donald Scherl. Ron Manderscheid of the National Institute of Mental Health provided statistics on the occupancy of state mental hospitals. Valuable advice was offered by Nancy Lombardo of the Alzheimer's Association, Gail Robinson of the Mental Health Policy Resource Center, and E. Clarke Ross of the National Association of State Mental Health Program Directors. Naturally, their advice does not imply the endorsement of this monograph by them or their associated institutions. The manuscript was prepared by Rita St. Pierre and Cathy Turnbull.

Introduction

The deinstitutionalization movement of the past three decades has profoundly altered the role of state and county mental hospitals in the care of elderly patients. Between 1972 and 1987, the proportion of Americans over 65 resident in public mental hospitals dropped from 374.6 per 100,000 to 67.6 per 100,000, an 82% decrease. Patients over 65 constituted 8% of all admissions in 1972, but only 4.5% in 1987, despite an increase in the number and proportion of older Americans during that interval.

Despite these dramatic changes, there remained in 1987 more than 20,000 elderly residents of state and county mental hospitals, who accounted for nearly one-fifth of all public mental hospital residents. Their care, costing well over $1 billion annually, is a major budgetary concern for the states. The quality of that care, and its impact on an especially vulnerable population of chronically mentally ill patients, deserves the concern of organized psychiatry.

In a number of states, the reduction of state mental hospitals' role in the care of mentally ill elderly patients has been the result of trans-institutionalization: the placement of elderly mentally ill patients in nursing homes rather than in hospitals. Transinstitutionalization has been a mixed blessing. On the positive side, it has enabled some chronically mentally ill elderly patients to live in more residential environments in or near their communities of origin. On the negative side, elderly mentally ill patients in nursing homes rarely receive the specialized mental health services they may need. Moreover, the cost of their care falls largely on the federal Medicaid program, a circumstance that has given rise to federal policies attempting to shift the cost of their care back to the states. The states, in turn, having their own fiscal problems and being responsible for the care of younger chronically mentally ill patients, understandably resist these cost-shifting efforts.

In the midst of the ongoing policy debate are the patients themselves and the dedicated individuals who assume the burden of their care. This task force report identifies and clarifies some of the clinical, administrative, and political dimensions of the care of elderly patients in state hospitals with the aim of enlightening the debate and assisting those striving to provide the best possible care in a time of constrained resources.

In approaching the problems of public sector mental health care of elderly patients, the Task Force chose to focus first on state mental hospitals, despite its awareness of a broadly held view that community-based care is the ideal and that there is a pressing need to develop other parts of the care continuum, including partial hospitals, sheltered housing, and outreach services. The focus of the Task Force on state hospital care was motivated by the following considerations: 1) there are many elderly patients in state mental hospitals who deserve better care than they get; 2) there is no immediately available alternative disposition for most of these patients; 3) large amounts of money are spent on the care of elderly patients in state mental hospitals, sometimes inefficiently and with disappointing results; 4) there is likely to be an enduring role for state-administered inpatient facilities in treating chronically and severely mentally ill patients, including mentally ill elderly patients; and 5) well-administered state hospital programs actually may help create a fuller continuum of care through educational and liaison activities, outreach programs, and collaborative arrangements with other providers of medical and mental health services.

The Task Force believes that the care of elderly patients in community mental health centers (CMHCs) is an issue deserving further detailed study. Although CMHCs are not discussed in detail in this report, a comprehensive public sector mental health policy for elderly patients would address for CMHCs the same issues explored here for state hospitals.

A common theme throughout this report is making the best of scarce resources. The Task Force shares the view with advocates for mentally ill patients that the total public sector commitment to mentally ill patients, including mentally ill elderly patients, is too small. In suggesting approaches to dealing with fiscal constraints, we presume, and actively participate in, continual advocacy of substantially increased public support for services for mentally ill patients, both young and old. In describing a minimal acceptable role for the state hospital in the care of mentally ill elderly patients, and in the care of dementia patients, the Task Force does not imply that improvement of hospitals is enough or that states should not go beyond a minimal role in their efforts to serve this population. Rather, the assertion is that the establishment of efficient, high-quality, and appropriately targeted state mental hospital services for elderly patients will aid in developing the political and administrative preconditions for further steps in the development of a comprehensive psychogeriatric care system.

In Chapters 1 and 2 of this volume, we begin by reviewing the history of care of elderly patients in state mental hospitals, available data about the current scope of the problem, and barriers to state hospitals' efforts to improve psychogeriatric services. In Chapter 3, we present the Task Force's consensus on ideals of psychogeriatric inpatient care that might be considered by those seeking to improve treatment. In Chapters 4 and 5, we discuss the roles of state hospitals in the care of elderly patients with primary mental illness and for patients with Alzheimer's disease and related disorders. In Chapter 6, we address the opportunities offered by state hospitals for training residents and fellows in geriatric psychiatry. Finally, in Chapter 7, we conclude with recommendations for action.

Chapter 1

History and Current Status of State Hospital Care of the Elderly

In this chapter, we review the history of state hospital care of elderly patients in this century and current developments that may affect the evolving role of the state hospital in their care. A comprehensive review of the history of mental health care of elderly patients is beyond the scope of this report. Overviews of the care of elderly patients in boarding homes, alms houses, and the early American asylums is provided elsewhere (Zwelling 1985).

Overview of 20th Century State Hospital Psychogeriatric Care

The decades between 1910 and 1950 witnessed an explosive growth in the census of geriatric patients. At the beginning of the century, the rate of state hospital admission for elderly patients was double that for younger patients. Between 1910 and 1950, the geriatric admission rate more than doubled, while the admission rate for younger patients remained stable. Thus by the middle of the century, elderly patients were being admitted to state hospitals four times faster than were their younger counterparts (Kahn 1975).

Most of these patients were not severely mentally ill and were admitted for some combination of medical, social, and economic reasons. Widespread admission of geriatric patients into state psychiatric hospitals occurred because there was no other system capable of providing long-term institutional care of frail or functionally impaired elderly individuals. Improvements in medical knowledge and treatment in the past five decades led to increased life expectancy among aging long-stay patients, who began to accumulate in large numbers in state hospitals, adding to the swelling ranks of the institutionalized elderly population (Sherwood and Mor 1980).

High mortality found among state hospital geriatric patients in the years following World War II led to heightened awareness of poor conditions in many state hospitals and to widespread dissatisfaction with institutional care. The passage of the Mental Health Study Act in 1955 (PL 84-182) authorized the formation of the Joint Commission on Mental Illness and Health in 1961, which published a book, *Action for Mental Health*. This book was strongly critical of the custodial care that was the norm in state hospitals. "Custodialism," the prevailing philosophy of care, yielded to an active treatment approach, driven in large part by the introduction of antipsychotic drugs.

As active treatment blossomed and long-term institutional care was decried for younger patients, the elderly were still seen by many as needing only custodial care. After the inception of Medicaid in 1965, many state systems transinstitutionalized some of their geriatric patients to nursing homes, which flourished in response to the demand for services made possible by the availability of federally assisted funding. Most nursing homes offered few mental health services, and behavioral rehabilitation for long-stay patients was rarely available. Geriatric units and medical infirmary services were developed in many state hospitals, but programs with identifiable treatment goals were lacking. Hence, custodial institutionalization remained the prevalent mode of care for mentally ill elderly patients. The historic revolution in American mental health care left behind the elderly population. The promise of community-based, rehabilitative treatment was not extended to them.

Deinstitutionalization and transinstitutionalization of the elderly population was also accelerated by changes in state hospital admission policies for geriatric patients. The tendency to treat elderly patients as a homogeneous group when planning services, and the widespread belief (still held today) that elderly patients were "dumped" into state hospitals not for active psychiatric treatment but for custodial care, led to the promulgation of admissions policies that were exceedingly restrictive (Epstein 1975). It was believed that diversion of geriatric admissions away from state hospitals could always be accomplished and was always clinically desirable. Thus between 1965 and 1987, the yearly geriatric admissions rate fell from 140,000 to 14,000.

During this time, however, an adequate system of noncustodial alternatives and community-based care failed to appear. During the 1970s, geriatric admissions to state hospitals fell by 55%, while admission rates for elderly patients to private psychiatric hospitals and nonfederal general hospitals increased only minimally (Department of Health and Human Services 1985). Nursing homes became the major institutional alternative, and they turned out to be more custodial than state hospitals ever were. Collectively, they had no mental health program policy, nor were they required to develop one (prior to the Omnibus Budget Reconciliation Act [OBRA] 1987). Burns and Taube (1990) recently have estimated that, based on 1985 National Nursing Home Survey data, less than 1 in 10 nursing home patients needing mental health services actually received them. Although their estimate of need may be spuriously high because not all patients with diagnosable mental disorders need specialized treatment, there is no doubt that there is an unmet need of considerable magnitude.

Amendments to the Social Security Act in 1965 that created Medicare (Title 18) and Medicaid (Title 19) provided mechanisms for funding psychiatric services to elderly patients in the community, but at rates that offered inadequate financial incentives to the private sector for treating nursing home patients. For example, until recently, the benefit for outpatient mental health services under Medicare was limited to $250 per year, after an effective 50% copayment, and provided no coverage for treatment by psychologists and clinical social workers. OBRA 1989 lifted the cap on reimbursement for outpatient mental health services and provided for direct reimbursement (with some restrictions) to psychologists and clinical social workers. However, the 50% copayment was retained for therapeutic services. This relatively high copayment, coupled with Medicare-allowed fees that may be well below prevailing fees, suggests that in many communities incentives for the private sector will remain insufficient for optimal service to nursing home residents.

Though there are admirable exceptions, community mental health centers (CMHCs) have been relatively unresponsive to the needs of elderly patients. The apparent reasons are both historical and financial. In the earlier years of the community mental health movement, many CMHCs focused on crisis intervention with younger adults, rather than the care of chronically ill patients. In recent years, CMHCs have responded to clear state directives to serve chronically mentally ill patients, but mentally ill elderly patients, and particularly those with comorbid physical illness, are not consistently seen as part of the targeted population. (In part, this reflects an appropriate concern of the National Alliance for the Mentally Ill [NAMI] and other advocacy groups that scarce public sector mental health dollars be focused on chronically and severely mentally ill patients. Older patients with dementia or with mixed medical and psychiatric problems often fall outside the rubric of "chronic and severe mental illness" even though their impairments may be both chronic and severe.) When service to the elderly population has not been part of a particular CMHC's historical mission, it may not be able to fund new efforts for elderly patients without taking resources away from other populations. Without new state funds for the care of elderly patients, and unwilling to "rob Peter to pay Paul," CMHC directors may reluctantly accept underservice of elderly patients even when they recognize the need. Although elderly patients were a specified population to be served by CMHCs, specialized psychogeriatric services were not in fact developed by many centers.

Without adequate alternatives, many geriatric patients remained in state hospitals. Data from Texas (Dittmar and Franklin 1980) suggest that the less difficult patients may have been transinstitutionalized to nursing homes, leaving state hospitals with the most difficult-to-treat elderly patients. Unfortunately, state hospital services for these patients remained preponderantly custodial in orientation. The myth that elderly patients do not respond to treatment became a self-fulfilling prophecy that biased the perception of the appropriate goals and role of psychogeriatric services (Moak 1988).

Current Status

Notwithstanding three decades of deinstitutionalization, elderly patients still account for about 19% of state hospital populations and 4.5% of new additions to these facilities. As recently as 1980, the state hospital accounted for 20% of all psychiatric hospitalizations of elderly patients (Milazzo-Sayre et al. 1987). The continued presence of elderly patients in state hospitals, despite deinstitutionalization, and future population demographic trends suggest that as long as there is a role for state hospitals in the mental health care system, a significant number of the patients are likely to be elderly. In the next two sections, we discuss quantitative estimates of geriatric patient populations in state hospitals, derived from National Institute of Mental Health (NIMH) statistics (National Institute of Mental Health, Survey and Reports Branch, Division of Biometry and Applied Sciences 1972, 1977, 1982, 1987). The trends are illustrated in Figures 1–1 through 1–4.

Secular Changes in Patient Populations Treated

The decrease in state hospital populations has been accompanied by a shift in the spectrum of diagnoses, away from organic mental disorders. (Most available statistics use the diagnoses "organic brain syndrome" and "organic mental disorders," and do not break out Alzheimer's and related dementias.) In 1972, 45% of all elderly inpatients in state hospitals carried

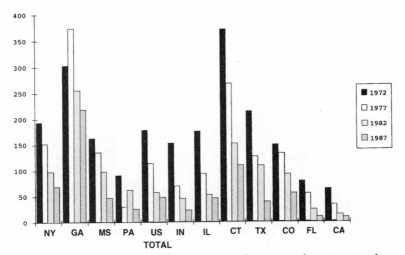

Figure 1–1. Proportion of individuals over 65 admitted to state and county mental hospitals (rate per 100,000 population). *Source.* National Institute of Mental Health, Survey and Reports Branch, Division of Biometry and Applied Sciences (1972, 1977, 1982, 1987).

the diagnosis of an organic brain syndrome, and 53.1% of all elderly admissions carried the diagnosis. Presumably, most of these patients had dementia. Persons with schizophrenia comprised 37.3% of elderly inpatients and 9.4% of admissions. By 1987, patients with organic brain syndrome comprised only 29.2% of elderly inpatients and 32.6% of admissions. Schizophrenia was the diagnosis in 43% of elderly inpatients and 19.9% of elderly admissions.

These data suggest that the primary focus of the state hospital and the care of the elderly has shifted to chronic or severe primary mental illnesses. Dementia care is now a secondary, but significant, role.

Heterogeneity Among States

Two main trends—the decreasing census and a smaller proportion of patients with organic mental syndromes—are virtually universal in the United States. However, the magnitude of these trends varies substantially from one state to another, as does the states' historical commitment to public sector treatment of mentally ill elderly patients. Some states have a

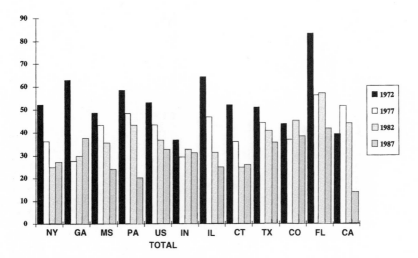

Figure 1–2. Percentage of patients over 65 admitted to state and county mental hospitals with "organic brain syndrome." *Source.* National Institute of Mental Health, Survey and Reports Branch, Division of Biometry and Applied Sciences (1972, 1977, 1982, 1987).

very large state mental health sector, and some continue to have large resident populations of patients with organic disorders.

For example, in 1987, New York had 340.8 per 100,000 of its overall elderly population resident in its state hospitals, whereas California had a rate of only 17.9 per 100,000. Thus there was nearly a 20-fold difference between states of comparable size and wealth. The difference between California and New York was of similar magnitude in 1972, suggesting that it is largely due to long-standing differences between state policies.

The proportion of elderly residents in state mental hospitals in 1987 was approximately 10% of the 1972 rate in Massachusetts, Ohio, and Pennsylvania, representing massive deinstitutionalization and trans-institutionalization in those states. By contrast, California, Connecticut, and New York had 1987 rates greater than 25% of the 1972 rates, suggesting a less rapid movement of patients.

The proportion of elderly state hospital residents with organic diagnoses also varied substantially between comparable states. In 1987, approximately 20% of all elderly state hospital residents had organic diagnoses in

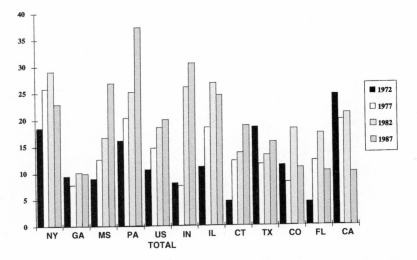

Figure 1–3. Percentage of patients over 65 admitted to state and county mental hospitals with "schizophrenia and related psychoses." *Source.* National Institute of Mental Health, Survey and Reports Branch, Division of Biometry and Applied Sciences (1972, 1977, 1982, 1987).

Florida and New York, whereas in New Jersey and Texas the rates were approximately 45%. New admissions with organic diagnoses comprised only 13.7% of all elderly admissions in California, but were 35.7% of new admissions in Texas and 32.3% in New Jersey.

These differences can be expected to underlie different states' reactions to federal policy initiatives for mentally ill elderly patients. States such as California, with a relatively small elderly state hospital population and relatively few dementia patients currently in state hospitals, could bear the brunt of any new federal mandates for a state hospital role in dementia care. For them, such a role would require a substantial commitment of new state resources. In states such as New York, with large existing commitments of state hospital resources for the elderly, important policy questions may center on the allocation of currently committed resources, rather than on expanding the present commitment.

Confusion over what types of services should be provided still plagues state hospital psychogeriatric services. Some authors (Barton 1983; Kobrynski and Miller 1970) have suggested that appropriate functions of state hospitals include 1) serving as backup for acute, private psychiatric

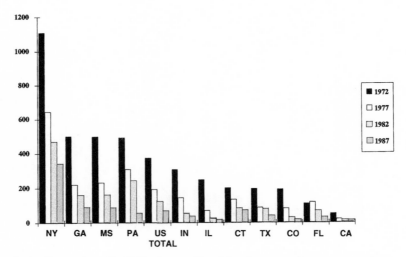

Figure 1–4.   Proportion of individuals over 65 resident in state and county mental hospitals (rate per 100,00 population). *Source.* National Institute of Mental Health, Survey and Reports Branch, Division of Biometry and Applied Sciences (1972, 1977, 1982, 1987).

hospitals, general hospitals, and nursing homes, for the most severe and persistent problems; 2) providing long-term care for treatment-resistant elderly patients who are not safely manageable in less restrictive settings; and 3) providing respite for the families of medically indigent elderly individuals who are in jeopardy of becoming institutionalized. What role state hospitals actually serve now is highly variable among states and has not been systematically examined. Further, a number of recent developments are likely to affect the evolving place of state hospitals in the continuum of care for the mentally ill elderly population.

Recent Developments Affecting Psychogeriatric Services

Foremost among the factors affecting state hospitals today are the shortcomings of CMHCs in responding to the needs of deinstitutionalized chronically mentally ill elderly patients. To a great extent, CMHCs never fulfilled their mandate under the Community Mental Health Center Act of 1963 (PL 88-164) to provide categorical services to the elderly population. In 1975, Congress passed the Community Mental Health Center Amendments (PL 94-63), which required CMHCs to provide services specifically for elders (and other special groups such as children). However, this law did not allocate additional funds for the newly mandated services. More recently, the adoption of block grants in 1980 as a new mechanism for funding CMHCs under the Alcohol, Drug, and Mental Health Administration (ADAMHA) has had a deleterious effect on CMHC services for elderly patients. Under block grant funding, previous requirements to serve categorical populations such as elderly patients have been eliminated. Data from one national survey of CMHCs (Flemming et al. 1986) show that the effect of this change has been to discourage some CMHCs from developing geriatric programs and to prompt others to drop existing programs. Thus historical shortcomings of many CMHCs were aggravated by fiscal constraints, which limited programs even in CMHCs that were positively committed to serving elderly patients.

At present, only 45% of CMHCs offer a geriatric program of any kind (Flemming et al. 1986). Little is known about the type or effectiveness of these services. It is known, however, that CMHCs have not been a major provider of services to nursing homes, or even to nursing homes with large numbers of transinstitutionalized mental patients. Growing recognition that for many chronically mentally ill patients nursing homes are nothing more than back wards in the community, more custodial than state hospitals ever were, has led to attempts to remedy these deficiencies through nursing home regulatory reform. New legislation promulgated under OBRA 1987 appears to represent the first step in this direction.

The Nursing Home Reform Act (OBRA 1987)

In 1987, Congress passed a comprehensive Nursing Home Reform Act, as part of OBRA 1987 (PL 100-203). A particularly controversial provision of the Nursing Home Reform Act was a provision requiring preadmission screening and annual resident review (PASARR) for residents with mental illness and mental retardation. In much of the recent literature on it, the PASARR provision is alternately, although inaccurately, referred to as the Nursing Home Reform Act, or as OBRA.

In brief, PASARR provides that patients entering nursing homes should be screened for primary mental illness. If they have a mental illness other than dementia or are mentally retarded, they require further screening to determine whether specialized mental health treatment or rehabilitative services are needed. If such services are needed, the patient must be sent to a facility capable of providing this specialized treatment. Patients currently resident in nursing homes must also be annually reviewed for the presence of mental illness or mental retardation and be sent to specialized facilities if the review determines the presence of a mental illness or mental retardation requiring specialized treatment. Of course, the patients are not eligible to remain in the nursing home in any case unless they have medical problems or functional disabilities that qualify them for Medicaid coverage. When PASARR revealed needs for mental health treatment not requiring a specialized mental health facility, the nursing home would be obliged to provide that treatment, although no additional funding would be available from federal sources, including Medicaid, to pay for such treatment.

The ostensible purpose of the PASARR provision was to prevent the inappropriate dumping of mentally ill and mentally retarded patients into nursing homes that could not provide needed therapeutic or rehabilitative services. However, there was also a cost-shifting agenda, in that the mental health treatment of nursing home patients was split out from the remainder of their general care and denied federal Medicaid reimbursement. States would thus pay the full costs of care for those excluded from nursing homes by PASARR and would have to support the mental health component of care for those not excluded but still needing mental health treatment.

Since the passage of this legislation, there have been many efforts to amend it, pursued through legislative, regulatory, and judicial channels. Nursing homes have sought either to weaken the provision or to get the federal government to underwrite more of the costs of screening and of providing needed services. State mental health authorities, charged by the provision with implementing screening, have been most concerned about additional costs and responsibilities imposed on state mental health systems by the law. OBRA 1990 included a number of technical amendments that increased the classes of patients excluded from complete screening and reduced the classes of patients for whom alternate dispositions are mandatory. As of 1990, PASARR applies only to persons with *serious mental illness* as defined by the Secretary of Health and Human Services in consultation with NIMH. Further, patients with a nonprimary diagnosis of dementia are now excluded from PASARR, as long as their primary diagnosis is not a "serious mental illness."

An estimate of the magnitude of the impact of the PASARR process is provided by a National Association of State Mental Health Program Directors survey (1990) of state mental health agencies on their 1989 experience with PASARR. In that year, 39 states reported a total of 31,296 Level II screens (full assessments) for patients identified by preliminary screening as possibly mentally ill. Elderly patients (age 65 and over) were the majority of those screened in most states. Thirty-seven states identified 2,839 persons in need of "active treatment for mental illness." This smaller number represents those patients for whom alternate dispositions would be needed or who would need active treatment in the nursing home at state expense. The number of individuals screened and the proportion deemed in need of active treatment varied greatly among states. Although on average about 9% of those screened were found to require active treatment, the proportion approached 50% in Oregon and was over 20% in California and Illinois.

A potential response to PASARR, under development in several states, is the development of state-funded mental health services that "wrap around" care rendered in nursing homes. Such care structures, should they come to fruition, would implement the true spirit of the PASARR law, which was to increase the likelihood that the mental health problems of nursing home residents would be treated. However, the PASARR experience, still unfolding, indicates the difficulty of bringing about such results through the rigidity of regulation rather than the flexibility of incentives. The jury is still out on its efficacy in improving the quality of mental health care for patients in nursing homes.

Other Provisions of OBRA 1987

In addition to requiring that nursing homes screen out mentally ill patients who do not require nursing care or who need intensive psychiatric treatment, OBRA 1987 requires that residents appropriately placed in nursing homes receive a full range of services to address their psychosocial needs and behavioral problems. This range of services is neither precisely defined nor funded by increases in Medicaid or Medicare reimbursement. Thus it is unlikely that nursing homes will be able to deliver all of the services described in the Nursing Home Reform Act to all elderly patients who need them. Nursing home beds are already in short supply (Swan 1987), and the gap between supply and demand threatens to grow with the explosion in the number of people over age 85, currently the fastest growing segment of the population with the highest risk of institutionalization. The introduction of prospective payment for reimbursement of acute general hospital inpatient services under Medicare has shortened hospital length of stay and increased the level of medical acuity among nursing home patients. For these reasons, and because new federal funds are not provided for the increased services required by the Nursing Home Reform Act, nursing homes may be reluctant to admit elderly state hospital patients. They may thus become more difficult to discharge from state hospitals (Swan 1987).

OBRA 1987 further mandated the development of regulations constraining the use of psychotropic drugs. As developed by the Health Care Financing Administration, these regulations provide that patients receiving neuroleptics must have a major psychiatric illness or must have an organic mental disorder accompanied by one or more of a list of specific target behaviors. The expected impact of these regulations is that less neuroleptics will be prescribed and that more psychiatric diagnoses will be made. Both of these consequences will lead to an increase in identified needs for mental health services for elderly patients in nursing homes.

State Initiatives to Decrease Hospitalization of Dementia Patients

Although OBRA may have the effect of keeping some elderly state hospital patients out of nursing homes, a recent development in Massachusetts suggests an approach that state mental health authorities might use to keep elderly patients with Alzheimer's disease and related disorders (ADRDs) out of state hospitals. The Massachusetts Department of Mental Health has promulgated regulations excluding ADRD patients (as well as all other patients with organic mental disorders) from being admitted to state mental health facilities (Massachusetts Department of Health 1988). This action appears to reflect a more generalized perception in government that ADRDs should not be viewed as mental illnesses (Governor's Task Force on Alzheimer's Disease and Related Disorders 1985).

Although this view was originally championed by advocates of dementia patients to destigmatize dementing diseases in Massachusetts, it has been exploited by the state mental health authority to decline responsibility for dementia patients, no matter how severe their behavioral disturbance. Depending on the state, this type of action could reduce admissions of geriatric patients by as much as 50%, while simultaneously creating new stresses on nursing homes and other chronic care facilities not under the auspices of mental health authorities. A similar policy, discouraging the development of inpatient beds for Alzheimer's disease patients in state mental hospitals, was adopted by the New York State Office of Mental Health (New York State Office of Mental Health, internal memorandum, 5 December 1988). The New York system has also undertaken specific efforts to transfer dementia patients not deemed dangerous to self or others to nursing homes, family care, or supervised adult homes (L. Campbell, New York State Office of Mental Health, personal communication, 7 January 1991).

Litigation

The system stresses implicit in the changes described here have given rise to several kinds of litigation. A number of suits were brought by the nursing home industry to delay the implementation of the PASARR provision of the Nursing Home Reform Act. These suits were successful in delaying the full implementation of preadmission screening and contributed to a regulatory weakening of the provision, which now permits the vast majority of mentally ill patients to remain in nursing homes as long as they are functionally impaired and do not have a current need for a hospital level of care.

A second type of litigation has been brought by the nursing home industry, concerned about the ever-increasing costs of meeting federal regulatory requirements that are not covered by an increase in state Medicaid rates. A recent federal court decision permitted nursing homes to bring suit against states if their Medicaid rates do not cover the costs of federally mandated services. This decision increases the likelihood that some of the increased mental health services required by the Nursing Home Reform Act will actually be provided, as it provides a mechanism for states to be forced to pay for them.

A third type of litigation comprises class actions seeking improved or alternative public sector mental health services for older people. Several such suits have been brought on behalf of mentally disabled individuals who claimed inappropriate institutionalization in state hospitals. For example, in *Brewster v. Dukakis* (D Mass, Consent Decree, 7 December 1978), the residents of Northampton State Hospital in Northampton, Massachusetts, sued for the creation of a range of community treatment alternatives for current and former residents of that facility:

> The consent decree specifically identified the needs of individuals over sixty-two years of age and required a special continuum of services for this population. As a result of the implementation of *Brewster* decree, the population of elderly individuals decreased from 115 (20% of the institution's census) to less than five. None of these individuals were transferred to nursing homes or other traditional long-term care settings. Instead, a range of community residential programs was created for them, several of which included significant nursing care and activities of daily living support components. Most of the individuals who left the hospital had been institutionalized for ten years or more. A follow-up study conducted by the Western Massachusetts Training Consortium documented that virtually none of the individuals were forced to return to the Northampton State Hospital. The

greater majority of them live safe and relatively productive lives and participate in many generic programs for the elderly. A few have been transferred to community general hospitals for treatment of acute and chronic problems. Several individuals died, although none from unexpected or accidental reasons. (S. J. Schwartz, personal communication, July 1990)

However, mental health advocates' enthusiasm for the Northampton State Hospital consent decree, as exemplified by the above quote, is not fully shared by public sector geriatric psychiatrists in Massachusetts. There are two main concerns raised by critics. The first is that clinically appropriate requests for readmission to Northampton State Hospital may have been refused since the consent decree took effect. The second is that community residences developed as alternatives might fail to meet treatment needs of residents and supply custodial care only. More detailed follow-up with extensive direct clinical assessment of the deinstitutionalized residents would be needed to fully answer these criticisms. Regardless, both sides agree that augmented community-based mental health services are needed to make deinstitutionalization more than the creation of community-based, decentralized "back wards."

In a similar settlement in Washington, DC—*Dixon v. Califano* (DDC, Consent Decree 1980)—the District of Columbia and the federal government agreed to improve conditions at St. Elizabeths Hospital. Part of the settlement focused on the needs of older residents of St. Elizabeths. As a result of pressure from the court, the District of Columbia developed plans to create a range of community services for former residents of St. Elizabeths.

A fourth type of litigation adopted by advocates for elders comprises damage claims on behalf of specific older individuals who received injury or harm while they were resident in state hospitals. A typical case from the state of Massachusetts is described in an April 1990 communication from Steven J. Schwartz of the Mental Health Protection Advocacy Project of the Center for Public Representation in Northampton, Massachusetts:

Galenski v. Noonan. This law suit was brought on behalf of a sixty-two year old man who had been institutionalized for over forty years, initially at the Northampton State Hospital in western Massachusetts and subsequently the Bridgewater State Hospital in southeastern Massachusetts. As a result of inadequate medical and psychiatric care, he was continuously restrained at Bridgewater and subsequently died by choking on solid food, despite a treatment plan that required him to be given only a pureed diet. The Commonwealth of Massachusetts has settled a portion of this litigation. The remaining action against the physicians for inappropriate medical care, inadequate psychiatric treatment, excessive restraint, the absence of any formal treatment planning, and grossly deficient emergency medical care remains pending. This suit, aimed at improving the policies and practices of the Bridgewater State Hospital, has already prompted a substantial modification of restraint procedures, particularly for elderly individuals. It has also resulted in a revision of the admission and treatment practices for this population. Finally, this and several other cases involving the deaths of Bridgewater residents have prompted the state legislature to significantly increase staffing and other resources for this facility.

These cases suggest that class action lawsuits will continue to serve as an engine for policy changes regarding public sector mental health. Litigation-driven reform may be encouraged by state legislatures' reluctance to commit new state funds to mental health programs unless forced to do so.

Conclusions

Despite the large-scale deinstitutionalization and transinstitutionalization of the elderly during the last three decades, geriatric patients still account for a large segment of residents in American state hospitals. State hospitals continue to be handicapped in their efforts to provide mental health care to elderly patients by a legacy of custodialism in psychogeriatric services and confusion about the appropriate role of the state hospital in geriatric mental health care. While deinstitutionalization of the elderly continues in many state systems, the growth of the elderly population, including those with severe and chronic mental illness, threatens to arrest if not reverse this trend. In addition to the increasing demand for inpatient services, legal pressure, community mental health center funding, and nursing home reform all are likely to affect the evolving role of state hospitals in the care of elderly patients.

Chapter 2

Barriers to Improving Care

Why have psychogeriatric services in state hospitals often been inadequate? The literature suggests that despite many states' substantial financial commitment and the energetic and dedicated efforts of hospitals' staffs, certain barriers have made the task more difficult (Gaitz 1974). These barriers include problems shared by all providers of health care to the elderly, as well as specific political and administrative problems of the public mental health sector.

Ageism in Psychiatry

Cultural and societal myths, prejudices, and stereotypes about old age, collectively referred to as *ageism,* pervade health care in general and psychiatry in particular (Butler 1969, 1975). In our society, mentally ill elderly individuals have the dual stigma of old age and mental illness (Talbott 1983). Ageism undermines recognition by the public, policy makers, and professionals alike of the legitimate health care needs of geriatric patients. One common manifestation of this phenomenon is the belief that psychopathology always represents an inevitable and untreatable concomitant of old age. Mental and emotional disorders of old age often are not recognized as bona fide mental illness requiring psychiatric diagnostic and treatment services.

The negative attitudes harbored by many clinicians toward the treatment of elderly patients (Ford and Sbordone 1980) and psychiatry's relative neglect of mentally ill elderly patients have been a further hardship for state hospitals (Butler 1969, 1975). Although inadequate standards of geriatric practice are now slowly yielding to the explosion of knowledge in

17

geriatric medicine and psychiatry, and to increasing social awareness of the graying of America, change is slow in many large systems. The gap between knowledge and practice appears to be especially wide in state hospitals. Prevailing views that custodial care is sufficient for geriatric patients often go unchallenged in public sector mental health systems. Commonly held myths that physical and mental dysfunction are inevitable and untreatable concomitants of aging reinforce the custodial orientation to care (Butler 1969, 1975).

Failures of Alternative Services

Psychogeriatric services have a low priority among state mental health planners: they ranked 30th among 62 policy concerns in a 1985 survey of state mental health commissioners. This low priority may result in part from the belief that alternative services in the community mental health centers (CMHCs), nursing homes, and senior centers and efforts by private providers would provide efficient mental health services and long-term care options for the elderly population. For a number of reasons, this has not happened.

Limitations of existing mental health care reimbursement under Medicare have been formidable obstacles to delivery of effective mental health services to elderly patients (Sharfstein 1990). Changes in the Health Care Financing Administration's guidelines for reimbursement of certain outpatient psychiatric services under Medicare, effective in 1988 and 1989, should enable some expansion of services to elderly patients. However, there are several reasons why even the recently increased Medicare psychiatric benefit will be unlikely to draw adequate numbers of private providers into the care of the mentally ill elderly population.

First, psychiatric care providers, both individual and institutional, often can fill their caseload with nonelderly patients. This is more true for psychiatrists than for providers of general adult medical services.

Second, both the individual and institutional providers usually are paid lower rates for their services by Medicare than their services can command in the open market. Psychiatric units in general hospitals either are subject to prospective payment under diagnostic related groups (DRGs) or are exempt from DRGs and reimbursed according to cost, but subject to an annual per-discharge cap. Free-standing DRG-exempt psychiatric hospitals also are subject to a per-discharge cap. Individual providers are paid rates that are usually lower than the full market rate for the same therapeutic services. In some states, such as Massachusetts and Rhode Island, acceptance of these lower rates is mandatory. In other states, maximum charges to Medicare patients are constrained by a maximum allowable annual charge (MAAC) that may also be less than the psychiatrists' current rate for non-Medicare patients. The Omnibus Budget Reconciliation Act of 1989 (OBRA 1989) will ultimately limit the MAAC to 115% of the Medicare charge.

Third, therapeutic services to outpatients are subject to a 50% copayment. Thus for an $80 therapeutic hour, the patient would directly be liable for $40. For most lower-income elderly patients, this effectively discourages treatment by a psychiatrist. For patients in nursing homes, the copayment often is essentially uncollectible.

Fourth, many activities incident to the psychiatric care of elderly patients are not covered at all or are difficult to bill for because of Medicare regulations and coding procedures. Such activities include telephone calls from patients and family members, liaison work with nursing home staff, and time spent coordinating medical and psychiatric care in conferences with other medical specialists involved in a patient's case. Although these activities are certainly part of general psychiatric practice for patients of all ages, they are especially frequent in geriatric practice because of the high level of medical comorbidity and active family involvement in caretaking.

Fifth, private sector inpatient care is further limited by lifetime limits on Medicare reimbursement for inpatient care in a psychiatric hospital or a designated psychiatric unit in a general hospital. An effective lifetime limit of 180 days translates into 9 days per year of hospitalization for a patient who lives 20 years after becoming eligible for Medicare at age 65. For patients with schizophrenia or severe recurrent mood disorders, this allowance may prove inadequate. Further, patients with dementia complicated by refractory behavioral problems can rapidly exhaust their lifetime days as well.

The combined effect of all of these considerations is that net hourly earnings are lower for psychogeriatric practice than for general adult psychiatric practice, controlling for other factors such as geographic region and socioeconomic status of the patient population. Also, private institutions have little incentive to develop psychogeriatric services if they can fill their beds with well-insured younger patients.

Older Americans have been low utilizers of mental health services in the community (Waxman 1986). As a result, most of the treatment they receive for mental health problems has been delivered by primary care physicians, who rarely refer geriatric patients to specialty mental health providers (Waxman and Carver 1984). Although the low utilization of conventional mental health services by elderly patients could be due to patient resistance, rather than provider neglect, substantial increases in mental health service use by older people have occurred when services were made available where older people live, when they were coordinated with general medical care, and when they involved little or no out-of-pocket cost. In San Francisco's On Lok program, which offered fully integrated community-based services paid for on a capitation basis without copayments, the major constraint on mental health services use was the availability of providers, rather than the reluctance of patients to seek treatment (Robinson 1990). Gene Cohen, deputy director of the National Institute on Aging, personally consulted to an elderly housing project for several years. Over the course of his involvement, use of on-site psychiatric services rose to 18% of the facility's residents (G. D. Cohen, personal communication, October 1988). In communities lacking such special programs—and they are the vast majority—optimal care for the more severe mental disorders of later life is difficult to obtain and may be delayed, to the detriment of both clinical and economic outcomes.

Patient Characteristics

State hospital psychogeriatric patients can be among the most difficult to treat of all inpatients. Many exhibit severely disturbed behavior, are severely functionally impaired, require substantial nursing care for age-associated physical problems, and can be resistant to care or even assaultive. Many are incompetent to consent to general health care, but lack guardians. Furthermore, most are poor. Their limited fiscal resources translate into limited dispositional options, contributing to longer lengths of stay and fostering pessimistic staff attitudes regarding patient treatment (Dawkins et al. 1984; Menninger 1984; Miller 1984; Moak 1988).

Geriatric patients may require architectural adaptations for sensory and mobility deficits and regularly require access to general medical care services often not found in state hospitals. Many state hospitals are not architecturally, programmatically, or administratively designed to facilitate the specialization and integration of services necessary for treatment of elderly patients or those with dementia (Talbott 1978). Deteriorating wards that are noisy, dark, drab, and monotonous are particularly adverse environments for confused, disoriented patients with cognitive and sensory impairments or physical disabilities. Operating budgets often lack provision to create barrier-free environments, special dietary and housekeeping services, extensive physical and occupational therapy programs, optimal environmental heating and cooling systems, accessibility to laboratory and radiological testing, and information systems to facilitate the efficient coordination of medical care, psychiatric care, and discharge planning.

The multiplicity of geriatric patients' needs can be overwhelming to service providers who are not prepared to provide the comprehensive services required. If providers have unrealistically high or inappropriately low goals for treatment, they may arrive at a sense of futility about treating elderly patients. Clinicians who have concluded that elderly patients rarely get better or cannot be helped by what they can offer are unlikely to get optimal therapeutic outcomes. In the worst case, inappropriately low standards of care are accepted, or elderly patients are denied treatment entirely.

Treatment for elderly patients in state hospitals is based on a high utilization of psychotropic medication and infrequent use of psychotherapy and formal behavioral therapy (McCarrick et al. 1988). "Custodial" treatment plans for geriatric patients are common (Moak 1988). For many newly admitted psychogeriatric patients, their inability to meet the functional demands of an institutional environment initially exacerbates behavioral problems. If the response is limited to neuroleptic medication and restraint, a vicious cycle may develop in which these patients become progressively less able to produce acceptable social behavior. Custodial institutionalization itself also may accelerate decline in the physical, and especially the instrumental, function of psychogeriatric patients. Skills not used may be lost.

Thus the contemporary portrait for geriatric care in state hospitals depicts an underserved, impoverished, and difficult-to-treat patient population, housed in limited or antiquated physical facilities. Caring for these patients makes extraordinary demands on both the clinical staff and the administrative structure of the state hospital. Although there are numerous dedicated individuals attempting to meet these demands, the overall picture suggests shortages of adequately trained personnel and administrative structures that at times limit creative solutions to clinical problems.

Personnel Limitations

The care of elderly state hospital patients has been particularly affected by declining physician involvement in public sector mental health services. Between 1974 and 1984, the proportion of psychiatrists and other physicians working in state hospitals decreased by 13% and 17%, respectively (Greene et al. 1986). The mental and behavioral problems of elderly patients are especially likely to be caused or aggravated by neurological problems. Those with primary mental disorders are highly likely to have comorbid medical illnesses, functional deficits, or sensory impairment. Thus services must be more multidisciplinary. Greater medical attention from both psychiatrists and other physicians is required, with important roles for physician extenders such as nurse clinical specialists and physicians' assistants. Moreover, rehabilitative disciplines such as occupational and physical therapy must be involved, with efforts coordinated by a coherent, comprehensive treatment plan. Although numerous disciplines are necessary for comprehensive care, adequate physician involvement is often crucial for a favorable outcome. For example, the most vigorous efforts of a physical therapist may be of no avail if a patient is stiff from excessive neuroleptics. Psychotherapy may be of little help to a melancholic patient who requires electroconvulsive therapy. And no mental health treatment by any discipline will correct primary medical problems that present as an aggravation of mental symptoms.

Unfortunately, there are relatively few well-trained geriatric psychiatrists or geriatricians willing to practice in state facilities. The lack of such specialists leads to multiple problems including diagnostic inaccuracy, vague treatment plans, inefficient team leadership, poorly planned services, and mismatching of services and needs. At worst, as occurred in the legal cases mentioned in Chapter 1, actual mortality may result from delays in detection and management of comorbid medical problems.

Quality care for geriatric patients requires successful integration of multiple disciplines, with clearly stated goals and objectives and effective leadership. This implies three related personnel requirements: 1) sufficient numbers of well-trained psychiatrists and geriatricians to address patients' medical needs; 2) physicians in leadership roles, with the interpersonal skills and attitudes necessary for effective collaboration with nonmedical professionals; and 3) leaders of other professional services (e.g., psychology, nursing, social work, occupational therapy, and physical therapy) with developed awareness of medical issues and with attitudes and interpersonal skills favorable to interdisciplinary collaboration.

Well-trained geriatricians and geriatric psychiatrists are in short supply. Equally important, leaders with collaborative skills and attitudes may be lacking even when numbers of staff are adequate. Miller (1984) noted the frequent resistance of lay administrators and nonmedical professional staff to physicians' attempts to provide leadership in state hospitals. Whether this can be ascribed to weaknesses of the nonphysician leaders or the would-be physician leader is uncertain, but the phenomenon Miller described is symptomatic of interdisciplinary conflicts that are all too common. Appropriate and effective sharing of responsibility among disciplines, with unambiguous physician responsibility for more medical aspects of treatment planning, requires both more highly skilled physicians and a sufficient number of institutional role models for collaboration.

Administrative Barriers

From an administrative perspective, the primary barrier for quality state hospital geriatric services is the low priority that both geriatrics and state hospitals receive among policy issues for state mental health directors (Ahr and Holcomb 1985). The low priority at the top translates to shortages of funds and, frequently, administrative neglect.

Some specific examples include the following:

1. Capital projects, for renovation of existing facilities or building new geriatric units, are given a low priority. Barrier-free environments, wheelchair-accessible bathing facilities, and motorized hospital beds improve patients' quality of life and reduce staff burden. Thoughtful

interior design can reduce the risk of falls and reduce disorientation in patients with dementia. Capital budgets for state hospitals have also suffered during deinstitutionalization, limiting capital improvement of existing facilities or the building of new specialized psychogeriatric units or hospitals. Between 1972 and 1981, the number of capital projects for public hospitals decreased disproportionately to other psychiatric hospitals (Checker 1986). Those projects that are undertaken have become more expensive and usually are financed by borrowed money. Given the current environment of fiscal restraint, only the highest priority capital projects (e.g., new prisons) are likely to receive public support. As a low-priority item even for state mental health program directors, state hospital psychogeriatric units are likely to remain undercapitalized for some time to come.

2. The bureaucratic structures of state hospital systems may interfere with flexible and efficient decision making. State hospitals are complex organizations, in which information management across departmental or committee boundaries may get distorted (Colenda 1986). Facility managers may feel caught between the Scylla of "management by committee," with its slowness and inefficiency, and the Charybdis of rigid, centralized authority. An organizational ideal would be delegation of program responsibilities from the central authority to hospitals and from hospitals to their operating units, with well-defined leadership, accountability, and semiautonomous control of resources at the operating unit level. This structure would permit, and even encourage, local innovations to solve emergent problems or serve special patient groups. Such structures, which mirror approaches in for-profit service industries, often contradict established bureaucratic traditions and could only be introduced with the full support of the highest levels of state government.

3. Community programs' claims on state mental health systems' fiscal and personnel resources may come at the expense of elderly patients, larger proportions of whom receive hospital rather than CMHC care. As long as state mental health systems are charged with the dual role of providing CMHC, as well as hospital, services, tension will exist in the system for the limited resources. Greater allocations to community care may come at the expense of elderly patients, unless CMHCs are committed to their care to the same extent that they are to the care of younger patients.

4. Quality assurance programs in state hospitals frequently fail to address common psychogeriatric concerns, such as efficient integration of medical and psychiatric care and a focus on functional assessment.

   Unfortunately, quality assurance programs themselves are vulnerable to the same barriers that undermine treatment of elderly patients. The ageist myths and therapeutic nihilism that plague treaters can also bias the assurers of quality. Efforts to assure quality of care for elderly patients will be ineffective if the appropriate standards for structure, process, and outcome are not adopted. Choosing the correct standards may be difficult, however, due to the heterogeneity of psychogeriatric patients (discussed further in Chapter 3).

Summary

In this review of personnel and administrative barriers to quality assurance, we emphasized geriatric services in state hospitals. In general these problems mirror systemwide problems for all patients in state hospital systems. A comprehensive effort to improve state hospital psychogeriatric services would need to deal with patients' needs for general geriatric care, staff needs for training and consultation, and managers' needs for adequate funding (including capital) and administrative flexibility.

Chapter 3

Principles of Treating State Hospital Psychogeriatric Patients

In this chapter, we enumerate principles of state hospital psychogeriatric treatment that offer a theoretical ideal for such care. Although the complete implementation of these principles is not possible, they are presented to assist in the identification of areas for improvement, according to a "continual improvement" model of change. State hospital programs have differing constraints, missions, designs, and case mixes. However, all can be improved, and we believe that many could identify promising initiatives within their existing administrative and fiscal constraints.

The Task Force hopes that the general principles set forth in the beginning of this chapter will be acceptable to a broad range of providers and advocates. The Task Force is aware, however, that its specific recommendations for improving care of elderly patients in state hospitals only represent informed opinion, rather than a definitive consensus or the conclusion of scientific studies. When specific schedules are set forth for periodic examinations and laboratory tests or when specific drug dosages are discussed, the recommendations are meant as guidelines for the form and substance of institutional quality assurance policies. Although general consensus on many of the issues addressed in this chapter is impossible until further scientific progress is made, the Task Force believes nonetheless that quality will be improved if institutions set standards based on their best informed judgment and modify them on the basis of further scientific progress and their own observed outcomes.

General Principles

Improving state hospital psychiatric care for the elderly mentally ill should be based on six major principles:

1. *Care for elderly mentally ill patients comprises good general geriatric care.* Compared with younger patients, whose psychiatric disability often can be attributed to a single cause, geriatric patients more often present with multiple, overlapping determinants of impairment. Organic mental disorders, such as dementia, delirium, and organic mood disorders, are far more frequent and commonly coexist with other psychiatric disorders, such as major depression or schizophrenia. Psychiatric decompensation commonly is precipitated by medical deterioration (Molnar and Fava 1987). Deterioration of vision, hearing, mobility, self-care, continence, or other functional capacities threaten independence and can lead to anxiety, depression, paranoia, confusion, or other symptoms that may lead to commitment to a state hospital.

   Comprehensive geriatric assessment by a multidisciplinary geriatric team represents an evolving technique in geriatric medicine (Verwoerdt and Eisdorfer 1967) that has clear applicability to the state hospital psychogeriatric treatment team. The cornerstone of this approach is multidimensional functional assessment followed by the simultaneous evaluation and treatment of all identifiable health problems in order to relieve symptoms, improve functioning, and enhance subjective well-being. This includes the identification and amelioration of common geriatric syndromes such as incontinence, immobility, and sensory impairment, as well as the implementation of preventive interventions recommended for elderly patients, such as influenza immunizations and sigmoidoscopy. To accomplish this, routine participation by various specialists such as podiatrists, dentists, audiologists, and medical subspecialists, including psychiatrists, neurologists, urologists, ophthalmologists, and others, is necessary. Program staff must be able to identify vision and hearing problems and procure eye glasses and hearing aids for patients with correctable deficits. Many patients may require physical therapy or speech therapy assessments, and some will need ongoing rehabilitative services. Difficulties that many elderly mental patients have in accessing the general health system, and in communicating their physical problems and needs, require that attention to general geriatric care be the responsibility of the psychiatric care provider.

The provision of good general geriatric care implies careful attention to the process of medical decision making for patients whose competence to make medical decisions is in question. Policies for informed consent and policies regarding advance directives for life-sustaining treatments deserve the same attention they would receive in a chronic care medical facility for elderly patients.

Nursing homes are required by the Omnibus Budget Reconciliation Act of 1990 (OBRA 1990) to inform patients and families of their rights to have advance directives; state hospital psychogeriatric services should do no less. However, a number of subtle issues must be considered in obtaining advance directives from mentally ill elderly patients in state hospitals. Competence to give advance directives is a specific issue that may be independent of the presence of psychosis or dementia; it hinges on patients having an adequate understanding of the particular issues of the proposed advance directive and the ability to determine and state a preference regarding those issues. As in the case of psychotic patients refusing medication, an individual with severe mental illness, and even thought disorder, might voice a desire to refuse a medical treatment for a sound and informed reason. On the other hand, most physicians would be reluctant to withhold basic medical treatment on the basis of an advance directive given by a profoundly depressed individual, even if that person were nominally competent.

Therefore, a state mental hospital's advance directive policy must be supported by a vigorous educational program for its professional staff and by procedural safeguards that might include diagnostic second opinions, consultation with legal counsel, and an active ethics committee. Buchanan and Brock (1989) have offered a recent and thorough presentation of ethical issues and procedural safeguards for surrogate decision making, including advance directives, involving both elderly and mentally ill patients.

2. *Improving care for elderly mentally ill patients depends on recognition of the heterogeneity of this patient group; different subgroups require different resources.* Three important subgroups of elderly state hospital patients are 1) patients with lifelong mental illness who have grown old in the state hospital; 2) patients with dementia complicated by psychosis, depression, or agitation; and 3) severely disabled patients with depression or anxiety

combined with chronic physical illness or functional impairment. Patients who have spent their entire adult lives in state hospitals may have different needs from those admitted for the first time in old age. Physically frail, dependent patients have different needs from functionally independent, well elderly patients. The "young old" (65 to 74), "old old" (75 to 84), and "oldest old" (85 and over) represent subgroups with different needs (Lazarus and Weinberg 1981). The tendency to plan and deliver services for elderly patients as though they represent a homogeneous patient population may impede improved care. Services naively thought to be appropriate for "the elderly" may be off-target with respect to the needs of the particular case mix of any single treatment program.

3. *A continuum of care must be provided to enable each patient to be treated in the setting that provides him or her with the greatest respect and independence.* The differing physical status and developmental stage of older psychiatric patients as compared with younger patients imply a need for specialized residential facilities and community support services. Neither the state hospital nor even the entire public mental health system is able to directly provide every part of the continuum of care. The services directly provided by the hospital will vary among and within states. At the policy level, the state must be committed to creating or facilitating the existence of all parts of the continuum, and at the individual level clinicians must continually seek the most appropriate treatment setting for each patient. Each agency's goals and limitations should be as clear as possible, so that both health planners and clinicians can see where the gaps are and avoid unrealistic expectations.

4. *Psychiatric care, particularly psychiatric care for elderly individuals with co-morbid physical illnesses or cognitive impairments, necessarily involves tradeoffs and compromises.* A well-known tradeoff is between safety and autonomy for the elderly person with wandering, intermittent confusion, and impaired gait. Although physical or chemical restraint may prevent falls (and even this is questionable), such restraints definitely will restrict autonomy. Letting patients walk freely respects their autonomy, but in some cases may increase the risk of injury. Another well-known tradeoff is between physical and chemical restraint. Physical restraints are more labor intensive and risk injury if incorrectly applied; chemical restraint by neuro-

leptics may limit mental autonomy and risk irreversible neurological complications, such as tardive dyskinesia. Moreover, restraints may lead to a loss of physical capacities due to disuse. Deinstitutionalization heightens the risk of noncompliance with medication and relapse of certain mental illnesses, yet usually offers a higher quality of life during intervals of relative remission of mental illness. Lower doses of neuroleptics may increase persistent positive symptoms or a rate of relapse in schizophrenia, but are associated with fewer neurological side effects and less dysphoria. Patients' preferences should be elicited and considered in deciding among treatment options.

5. *Much of the care of elderly mentally ill patients is rendered by family caretakers; the incorporation of these caretakers into the treatment planning process, respect for their opinions, and provision for their needs for assistance, support, and respite are also part of an ideal system.* In some cases, the family caregiver, rather than the identified patient, may become the primary consumer of services.

6. *Behavioral emergencies in elderly patients may represent acute physical illness, acute or exacerbated mental illness, or some combination of the two.* Therefore, psychiatric emergency and crisis management services for elderly patients must be fully integrated with acute medical care, and emergency evaluations should always include a thorough medical reevaluation.

Specific Approaches to Improving Treatment of Elderly State Hospital Patients

A. Diagnosis

1. All patients should have accurate DSM-III-R diagnoses. Old diagnoses made according to prior diagnostic criteria, or without regard to any formal diagnostic criteria, should not be recognized as accurate. Diagnoses of long-stay patients should be reviewed annually, with confirmation of diagnosis by outside consultants on a selected sample of patients.

2. Any chronically hospitalized patient who has an acute or subacute change in mental state, not consistent with his or her known mental illness, should

receive a diagnostic reevaluation by a physician that specifically includes acute and subacute organic disorders in the differential diagnosis and rules them out with appropriate technology.

3. All patients should receive a functional assessment, including standard measures of activities of daily living (ADLs) and of cognitive performance. For example, more impaired patients could receive the Katz Index of Activities of Daily Living, whereas less impaired patients could receive the Extended Katz Scale (e.g., ADLs plus shopping and transportation), or portions of the Philadelphia Geriatric Center Multi-Level Assessment Instrument. Testing of cognitive function might employ an instrument such as the Cognitive Capacity Screening Examination or the Mini-Mental State Exam; patients reaching a ceiling performance on one of these tests should receive a more sensitive instrument so that early and subtle dementing illnesses can be properly detected. Vision and hearing should be formally tested, ideally with an optometric examination and audiometry, but at least with screening measures to establish that vision and hearing are adequate for reading and verbal communication. Formal occupational therapy assessment should be performed, and can be designed so that ADL measurements are obtained concurrently. A physical therapy evaluation should be performed on all patients with physical handicaps that impairm physical or instrumental ADLs, particularly mobility.

In regard to functional assessment, state hospital psychogeriatric patients should receive no less than the Minimum Data Set (MDS) mandated by OBRA 1987 for the assessment of all residents of Medicare- and Medicaid-certified nursing homes (Morris et al. 1990). MDS includes sections on cognition, communication and hearing, vision, physical function, consonants, psychosocial well-being, mood and behavior, activity pursuit, disease diagnoses, health conditions, nutritional status, dental status, skin conditions, medication use, and special treatments and procedures.

4. Ratings of physical function, cognitive performance, hearing, and vision should be repeated at least annually; significant deterioration should trigger an appropriate medical evaluation of the reason for increased impairment.

5. Any patient with excessive daytime somnolence, insomnia, or nocturnal disruptive behavior or any patient requiring regular medication for sleep

should have a specific evaluation of the sleep complaint. A DSM-III-R sleep disorder diagnosis should be attempted if the sleep disturbance is not explained by a diagnosed medical or psychiatric disorder.

6. All patients should have an evaluation for abnormal involuntary movements that includes use of the Abnormal Involuntary Movement Scale (AIMS) or a similar instrument. All disorders of posture and movement should be noted in the medical record, as should tremors, involuntary movements, or impaired coordination. Neurological consultation should be obtained when a motor disorder impairs the patient's everyday function, and evaluation by the attending psychiatrist and/or general physician has not led to a definite diagnosis and plan of treatment or management. The motor system should be reevaluated at least annually and more frequently if the patient is undergoing medication changes that may influence the motor system.

7. Any patient with impairment in gait should receive a medical or neurological evaluation adequate to diagnose the cause and contributing factors and to suggest a plan for remediation. Formal subspecialty consultation is often indicated if the impairment significantly reduces the patient's mobility or has led to repeated falls, and medical and neurological evaluations by the attending psychiatrist and/or medical generalist have not resolved the diagnostic and therapeutic issues.

8. Any patient with urinary or fecal incontinence should have an adequate medical or urological evaluation to determine the cause and to identify remediable causes.

B. Treatment Plan

1. The treatment plan must specifically address psychiatric problems, general medical problems, neurological diseases, functional impairments, and social problems; a plan should be provided for each.

2. The treatment plan should have specific goals, one of which will always be the preservation or improvement of independent function. (An equivalent concept is the prevention and amelioration of "excess disability," that is

those impairments not a necessary and invariable consequence of the patient's medical condition.)

3. When appropriate, treatment plans should specify advance directives regarding life-sustaining treatment should the patient deteriorate medically. Although it is expected that patients with life-threatening medical problems could be transferred to acute care medical facilities, a transfer might come too late for discussions of patients' wishes and preferences.

   Facilities' policies regarding advance directives should take into account the ethical complexities of soliciting information on patients' preferences. Patients in state mental hospitals, if competent, have the same rights as other people to express their intentions through living wills or durable powers of attorney. However, they must be protected from subtle institutional pressures to forego future treatment.

C. Placement

1. Discharge from the hospital should be an initial goal of treatment for every elderly state hospital patient. Those patients who, despite aggressive and persistent efforts at treatment, remain too disturbed or dangerous to be managed outside of a locked psychiatric setting, may constitute a group of long-stay patients for whom discharge is not realistic. Identification of a patient as appropriate for a long hospital stay should be justified by a careful analysis of the patient's disabilities and thorough consideration of potential resources for treatment in a less restrictive setting. Patients in this group who are presumed to be impossible to discharge should be reviewed regularly, as changes associated with aging or physical disability might make a locked psychiatric unit unnecessary even if the primary mental illness does not remit. Second opinions from outside consultants should be sought for such patients.

2. Patients' comprehensive treatment plans should identify specific problems that, if resolved, would permit discharge to a less restrictive setting. Examples of such problems are violence and aggression, mobility problems, communication problems, and medical noncompliance. The treatment plan should identify environmental resources and services necessary to permit placement in a nonhospital setting once these problems are resolved.

3. Patients' need for continuing hospitalization should be reassessed once every quarter, and the conclusion of the assessment should be expressed in terms of problems remaining to be solved or community services necessary for successful outplacement, even if not currently available.

D. Relations With the Community

1. The facility should offer educational programs for the community and for local medical practitioners on the recognition and management of mental illness in elderly individuals. Community providers should be periodically updated on the role of the state hospital psychogeriatric service in the continuum of services available in the community, the services offered by the program, and how to access them.

2. The facility should respond within one working day to inquiries from families and health care providers about services offered by the facility. The facility should direct callers to the appropriate source for services or information not provided by the facility.

3. Facility staff should work with nursing home and/or board-and-care operators to develop environments for deinstitutionalized patients.

4. The facility or affiliated community mental health centers should provide a home visit service with authority to arrange hospitalization when severe mental illness unmanageable in the community is discovered.

5. The facility should provide instruction and advice to family caregivers who will be taking full or partial responsibility for deinstitutionalized patients.

6. Legal services should be available to patients and their guardians, provided by legal staff familiar with legal issues specific to old age, dementia, and mixed physical and mental disability.

E. General Management

1. Every effort should be made to modify the physical plant to accommodate the needs of the geriatric case mix being served. Necessary architectural

modifications may include ramps, handrails, and wider doorways to facilitate handicapped and wheelchair access. Allocating more floor space per patient may be necessary in settings that serve frail, handicapped patients. Some bathrooms and showers need to be wheelchair accessible. Floors should be nonslip and nonskid and might be carpeted, depending on the case mix. Special attention to lighting, acoustics, and color scheme is important for patients with cognitive or sensory impairments. Furniture designed to reduce falls and improve mealtime posture may be required. Ground-level egress from inpatient units to the outdoors is helpful for frail, disabled patients, and direct access to an enclosed, safe, outdoor area is helpful for cognitively impaired patients who wander. Consultation can be obtained from specialists in the architectural and interior design needs of geriatric patients.

2. Prostheses, canes, walkers, hearing aids, properly fitting dentures, and eyeglasses should be readily available and be promptly replaced if lost or damaged.

3. Civil commitment status, competence, and the need for guardianship should be reviewed at least annually. When a patient is stated in the medical record to be incompetent, the reason for incompetence should be specified and should be redocumented at least annually. The record should state whether there is a guardian appointed or the appointment of a guardian is in process. Efforts should be made to obtain a guardian as rapidly as possible for any patient likely to remain incompetent. (*Incompetence* here refers to the inability to make health care decisions because of mental impairment, viewed as a clinical determination. The legal determination of incompetence implies the appointment of a substitute decision maker.) Assessment of competence is appropriate even when patients are on voluntary status, because they may have competently signed into the hospital many years before the present evaluation. Appointment of a guardian is in some cases a necessary condition for community placement.

4. When physical or chemical restraints are used to prevent wandering, falls, or injuries to patients or staff, the need for restraints should be regularly reevaluated, and tradeoffs between the risks and putative benefits of restraints should be explicitly considered and documented in the medical record.

F. Health Maintenance[1]

1. All female patients should have an annual breast examination plus mammograms when clinically indicated.

2. All female patients should have a baseline Pap smear and pelvic examination, with follow-up examinations on a schedule to be determined by the gynecologist based on risk factors and past history.

3. All patients should have a baseline sigmoidoscopy and annual examination of stool for occult blood, with follow-up sigmoidoscopy when indicated.

4. All male patients should have a rectal examination annually to screen for carcinoma of the prostate and rectal carcinoma.

5. Smokers should be advised to quit, and a smoking cessation program should be available for all patients.

6. Patients should receive an annual blood count, and a medical workup for anemia should be undertaken for any anemic patient.

7. All patients with macrocytosis should have a B_{12} level test; B_{12} level tests should be done annually for all patients with a history of gastrectomy who are not already receiving B_{12} supplementation.

8. Multivitamins should be given daily to all patients, unless a patient's dietary history establishes an adequate and consistent intake of vitamin requirements.

9. Examinations for abnormal involuntary movements should be conducted and recorded twice a year for all patients on neuroleptic therapy.

10. Patients should be weighed at least once a month, with a medical reevalua-

---

[1] *Note:* Some of these recommendations may be inapplicable to patients with end-stage dementia.

tion for any clinically significant weight gain or loss over the previous month. (If the weight gain or loss was the desirable result of a therapeutic intervention, the appropriate evaluation might be limited to assessing the patient's progress and determining the need for continued dietary intervention.)

11. Any fall should trigger a neurological examination, assessment of orthostatic vital signs, and reevaluation of the patient's medication list. Blood levels of medications should be obtained when clinically indicated.

12. Patients should be screened annually for swallowing disorders that might raise a risk of choking or aspiration. If a swallowing disorder is identified on screening, the patient should be medically evaluated to establish a diagnosis, plan for remediation, and appropriate diet.

13. All patients should have an annual physical examination and detailed review of systems, directed at identifying new medical conditions that have developed during the past year, particularly those that require treatment. When a patient has dementia or is unable to communicate, family members or ward staff who know the patient best should be systematically questioned about the patient's symptoms or changes in status.

14. All patients over 40 years old should have an electrocardiogram in their medical record. Patients over 40 years old receiving psychotropic medications with cardiac effects, such as phenothiazines, tricyclic antidepressants, and lithium, should receive an annual electrocardiogram. Significant changes in the electrocardiogram should be addressed by a medical consultation.

G. Medication Use

1. All psychotropic medications should be related in the medical record to specific mental disorder diagnoses and/or specific target symptoms. If a patient arrives at the state hospital on a psychotropic medication that does not clearly relate to a mental disorder diagnosis, the issue should be clarified and documented within 1 week.

2. Antipsychotic drug dosages for the treatment of psychotic disorders should be minimized. Any elderly person receiving the equivalent of more than 500 milligrams of chlorpromazine per day of an antipsychotic drug should have an effort made to reduce the dosage, unless there is well-documented evidence that this was attempted in the past and was found unsuccessful because of a relapse of mental symptoms.

3. Any patient on an antipsychotic drug with tardive dyskinesia or other neurological side effects directly related to antipsychotic drugs, such as parkinsonism, should receive a trial of dosage reduction unless it is well documented that previous well-planned attempts at dosage reduction were unsuccessful. The patient's records should reflect that efforts were made to reduce the dose to the absolute minimum necessary to control target symptoms. The issue of antipsychotic drug dosage should be reviewed at least twice annually. If there are compelling reasons not to reattempt a reduction in dosage, such as persistent positive symptoms or a compelling history of early relapse when drugs were reduced, these reasons should be documented.

4. When a patient is receiving the equivalent of 100 milligrams of chlorpromazine or more of an antipsychotic drug for an indication other than a psychotic disorder (e.g., agitation), efforts should be made to substitute a nonneuroleptic alternative medication for the same target symptoms. These efforts should be made at least twice a year; if repeated and unsuccessful, or if there are relevant medical contraindications to neuroleptic alternatives, reasons for continued neuroleptic use for a nonpsychotic indication should be documented in the medical record.

5. A patient should not be on two or more drugs of the same psychotropic drug class, unless there is a sound, specific, and adequately documented reason for the choice.

6. Each patient's entire drug regimen should be systematically reviewed quarterly.

7. A patient receiving regular hypnotic medications for more than 3 months should be evaluated for sleep disorder.

8. When a patient has been receiving benzodiazepines or sedative drugs for more than 6 months on a daily basis, a determination should be made as to whether the benzodiazepines are primary and appropriate treatment for an anxiety disorder or they are being continued because of the patient's physiological dependence on the drug. If there is no compelling psychiatric or medical indication for continuing the benzodiazepine, a plan for appropriate and gradual withdrawal should be implemented.

9. If a patient is receiving a tricyclic antidepressant, an electrocardiogram while the patient is on the current dosage of the drug should be obtained and be available in the record. A patient to be newly begun on tricyclics should have a baseline electrocardiogram. If there are abnormalities but they do not contraindicate treatment, a schedule should be specified for monitoring electrocardiograms during dosage titration.

10. If a patient is receiving a tricyclic and has not had a full remission of depression after 2 months of drug treatment, a blood level should be obtained to determine adequacy of dosage. If the patient is having a good therapeutic response to a tertiary amine tricyclic but has significant anticholinergic or orthostatic side effects, efforts should be made to substitute an alternate antidepressant with fewer of these side effects, for example a secondary amine agent, bupropion, or fluoxetine.

11. If a patient is receiving a psychotropic together with medications prescribed for concurrent medical illness, the patient should be screened for potential drug interactions using a current reference or data base, such as the *PDR Drug Interactions and Side Effects System* (1989). If the patient is at risk, appropriate clinical assessment for drug interactions should be undertaken. This may include drug levels. All patients receiving a psychotropic drug should receive a psychiatric reevaluation for efficacy, side effects, and appropriateness of drug continuation at least once per quarter.

12. Patients on an antipsychotic drug with significant gait disturbance due to parkinsonian side effects should receive a trial of antiparkinson medication. If antiparkinson mediation of one class (e.g., anticholinergic) is not tolerated or is not effective, antiparkinson medication of an alternate class (e.g., antihistamine and dopamine agonist) should be tried.

13. Elderly patients on lithium should receive a pre-lithium evaluation to include electrolyte levels, blood urea nitrogen and creatinine levels, a thyroid-stimulating hormone level, and an electrocardiogram. Patients on lithium should have repeat testing of renal function and thyroid function once per quarter.

14. Patients who develop new onset incontinence while on lithium should be evaluated for lithium-induced diabetes insipidus. If this complication is present, it should be actively managed by substituting an alternate antimanic drug, by reducing the lithium level or dosage frequency, or by coadministering an appropriate diuretic under medical supervision. Efforts should be made to restore continence in such patients.

15. When patients are first admitted to the facility, a complete drug profile should be obtained, either from their family or the professional caretaker most recently involved with the patients. An inspection of the contents of the medication cabinet is desirable.

16. Before discharge from the facility, a written medication list should be discussed with patients, their family, their professional caretakers, and their primary care physician. Special requirements for dosage, diet, and monitoring for side effects should be imparted specifically to all members of the treatment network, both professional and nonprofessional.

H. The Therapeutic Milieu

The therapeutic milieu should provide dignity and respect, and engender a sense of autonomy to combat chronic long-stay patients' sense of being warehoused, waiting to die, and to create among acute patients expectations of improvement and of prosocial, independent behavior. The therapeutic milieu must integrate elements of both the psychotherapeutic environment needed by mentally ill patients and the rehabilitative environment needed by functionally impaired elderly patients. Adaptation of the milieu to different patient populations (e.g., chronic versus acute illness and dementia patients versus non-dementia patients) might be facilitated by grouping similar patients on different wards or subunits. This integration is essential to the overlapping tasks in this patient population of improving functional ability or, at least, compensating for unremediable disability, while encouraging prosocial behaviors and general motivation.

1. The milieu should employ systematic reality orientation for psychotic or cognitively impaired patients.

2. Staff should encourage independent self-care to the greatest extent possible. Staff should provide assistance with ADLs to the extent needed by each patient based on an evaluation of the patient's abilities. Cuing and supervising patients generally should be preferred to staff doing the task.

3. A token economy system should be considered for patients with the cognitive capacity to respond to it. Real reinforcers, such as an actual paycheck, even if nominal, for participation in a work rehabilitation program, may be more useful. Token economy programs should be implemented with consent of the patients, if they are competent.

4. The activities program should expose patients to a range of occupational and social activities to make life in the institution more enjoyable, to develop social skills, and, ultimately, to facilitate function in a less restrictive environment. Activities might include social dancing, bingo, movies (on video), community outings, cooking groups, outdoor or indoor gardening, music, and exercise.

5. With respect to living space and milieu activities, it may be helpful to cluster patients according to functional abilities. Programs jointly involving male and female patients are as important to older patients as to younger ones. Program staff should be prepared to handle both normal and abnormal sexual behavior among the patients.

6. Bedtime hours should be flexible for patients desiring to stay up in the evening (particularly for elderly patients, who ordinarily require less sleep than younger patients and often sleep less at night). Late evening relaxation groups should be considered if initial insomnia is a widespread problem.

7. Group meals should be supervised by the staff to provide a pleasant, socializing experience. Observation of patients for problems with swallowing or with drinking can be carried out unobtrusively at these times.

8. Each patient should have a specific staff member designated to monitor and encourage his or her participation in activities and to help plan his or her daily routine.

Quality Assurance in Geriatric Psychiatry

Quality assurance has been suggested as one methodology for specifically improving health care organizations' responsiveness to common geriatric problems (Fink et al. 1987). Well-designed quality assurance programs might help bridge the gap between the knowledge base of geriatric psychiatry and existing standards of practice.

Zusman (1988) and others (e.g., Galasso 1987) suggest that the establishment of effective quality assurance standards requires answers to empirical questions (Do quality of care standards improve quality?) and development of practical guidelines. For psychogeriatric services, these fundamental questions are difficult. Many quality assurance standards are "process" oriented, measuring, for example, patient attendance at activity sessions or even orders for activity therapy, as opposed to health outcome oriented, directly rating changes in patients' behavior. Measures of outcome offer the advantages of encouraging creativity and flexibility in process and facilitating continual improvement, but outcome measures are technically difficult. The outcome measures to be used must be shown reliable in the hands of those who will use them and must meet external criteria of validity. Despite these challenges, the Health Care Financing Administration has committed itself to developing an outcome-based approach to nursing home quality assurance and has invested several million dollars in the first step of developing a uniform MDS for resident assessment. The MDS has sufficient data on cognitive, behavioral, and physical function to permit the detection of changes, both positive and negative, that may result from the care rendered.

Prevalent quality of care standards comprise some combination of structure, process, and outcome criteria. In this chapter, we have concentrated on process and suggested some outcomes that might be measured as a step toward a greater outcome orientation. The MDS for nursing home residents might also deserve testing and possible adaptation for use on state hospital psychogeriatric services. Although many general features of structure are addressed by the Joint Commission on Accreditation of Health-care Organizations, its standards may require some modification or augmentation for psychogeriatric services. Moreover, the appropriate structure for community services, medical consulting services, laboratory services, and so on, may vary according to the size of the facility, the nature of the community served, and the resources available. It is premature to specify specific outcomes to be attained; a necessary first step is the collection of accurate diagnoses and outcome data from a number of facilities. This would permit the development of statistical norms for outcomes and the recognition of excellence and deficiency.

In treating elderly mentally ill patients, it is often impossible to simultaneously maximize physical function, cognitive function, freedom from psychiatric symptoms, safety, and autonomy, necessitating "tradeoffs" with regard to these various dimensions of outcomes. Making tradeoffs of this kind is one of the most difficult tasks both for the individual clinician and for the psychiatric institution; appropriate outcome-based quality measures may ultimately help institutions with this problem. (Eliciting patients' preferences is also a necessary part of the decision-making process.) Within an institution, outcome-based quality measures might identify policy changes leading to unacceptably higher rates of adverse outcomes. If applied consistently by many institutions, such measures would allow the distinction of poor quality care from the acceptance of an appropriate tradeoff.

For example, suppose a number of institutions consistently measured the rate of falls and the use of restraints for a defined geropsychiatric population. A scatter plot could be produced that would permit the determination of an "acceptable" rate of falls given a particular level of use of restraints. An institution significantly higher than the norm both on falls and on the use of restraints, controlling for the severity of its patients' gait problems, would be identified as having a probable quality of care problem. An institution with a relatively low rate of both could be examined as a potential model of care quality. Data on outcomes and tradeoffs from a number of hospitals would also be helpful in responding to administrative and legal pressures to go to extremes in the pursuit of safety or of patient autonomy by providing an objective measure of the consequences of such policies.

Quality assurance, particularly using outcome-based measures, has been termed *the third revolution in medicine*. Given the extraordinary costs of institutional care of chronically mentally ill patients, and the legal and ethical dilemmas presented by such care, the care of elderly mentally ill patients in state hospitals should be a very rewarding area for innovation in outcome-based quality assurance.

Comments on Process Recommendations and Outcome Measures

The central problem of quality assurance in psychogeriatrics is that the relationship between the process of care and its outcome is unknown for many clinical conditions and patient care procedures. Although we suggest criteria for the process of diagnosis and treatment that enjoy broad consensus among academic geriatric psychiatrists, proof is lacking to connect most of these process recommendations with the desired outcomes of better function, less restrictive environments, fewer adverse reactions to drugs, and so on. Therefore, an essential feature of implementation of these recommendations is the establishment of systematic data collection on outcomes within state hospitals. If, for example, functional status is not systematically measured, there is no way to determine whether occupational and physical therapy interventions improve function. If adverse drug reactions are never reported, it is difficult to use the rate of such reactions as a measure of the success of periodic reviews of patients' drug regimens.

The task of instituting meaningful outcome measurement and developing a data management system to meaningfully analyze outcome statistics is formidable. Nonetheless, if a state hospital has a computer system used for billing and other administrative purposes, it has the hardware to develop such a system, if there is an institutional commitment to doing so. Moreover, ongoing work on computerized analysis of MDS data from nursing homes may help develop suitable methodology for practical outcome measurement in long-term care. In our opinion, the commitment to tracking at least some of the outcome measures suggested in this document is a crucial initial step toward improved care quality.

Widespread introduction of systematic outcome measurement as we have described would offer two additional benefits. First, it would enable the identification of hospitals with particularly successful programs that might be used as models for other institutions. Second, it would permit an explicit analysis of difficult tradeoffs, as described above. This analysis could be useful to institutions addressing legal and political pressures to overemphasize one dimension of quality at the expense of another.

Chapter 4

Role of the State Hospital in the Care of Mentally Ill Elderly Patients

Public sector mental health systems are the primary source of care for chronically mentally ill patients, and a gap filler in the care system for dementia patients and elderly patients with acute psychiatric problems. These latter groups are referred to public mental health systems if they are indigent, if they are violent, or if they require involuntary treatment. Treating these latter groups of patients requires effective coordination of care rendered in the public sector with care rendered by the general health system.

Recent work on chronic mental illness in elderly patients, paralleling earlier work on chronic mental illness in younger populations, suggests that community-based care properly matched to patient needs reduces hospital days and leads to an overall cost no greater than hospital care, while affording patients greater autonomy.

Although there is little disagreement that the public sector has a role in the care of elderly patients with primary mental illness (nondementia) and that community-based care is preferable when possible, there are substantial impediments to translating this approach into reality. Among them are the separation of fiscal and administrative responsibility for inpatient versus community-based services for mentally ill elderly patients, the separation of fiscal and administrative responsibility for psychiatric and general medical care, and inadequate funding of housing and community services in many localities. We address these issues later in this chapter.

Difficulties in realizing the ideal of short-term hospital treatment for chronically mentally ill patients may indirectly diminish the efficacy and efficiency for acutely mentally ill patients as well. If a hospital has a large proportion of long-stay patients, both staff and patients may develop negative expectations about the outcome of treatment. If a patient with an acute agitated depression is referred to the state hospital because of violence, suicide potential, or a lack of resources (e.g., no remaining Medicare coverage), the patient ideally should receive a rapid medical and neurological assessment, followed by aggressive trials of medication or electroconvulsive therapy, and psychosocial therapies oriented toward the restoration of morale and function. If the patient was placed on a ward with many long-stay patients, staff with generally pessimistic expectations regarding recovery, slow-paced medical work-ups, few psychosocial treatments, and reluctance to aggressively pursue specific biologic treatments, the likelihood of a rapid remission would be substantially lower. Some patients would go on to have chronic illness, whereas others might eventually remit at a slower pace than would have been possible with optimal acute treatment. Delays in remission due to suboptimal treatment involve costs to both the institution and the individual. Not only does the state have to pay more for a longer hospital stay, but the individual may suffer a loss of housing, social relationships, and integration with the community that may have long-term deleterious effects on his or her function and well-being.

The Task Force report supports an interim policy of developing acute treatment units within state hospitals, specifically to provide aggressive short-term treatment to patients with acute or recently relapsed psychiatric illnesses. Even if systemic changes cannot be made to provide effective short-term treatment for all state hospital psychogeriatric patients, efforts should be made to insulate acutely ill patients from becoming demoralized by a custodial approach to care. Of course, continuing efforts must be made to reduce the custodial approach for all long-term care patients.

Integration of Hospital and Community Care

Patients with chronic mental illness, particularly schizophrenia, have a combination of positive symptoms and negative or deficit symptoms.

When acute hospital treatment has succeeded in attenuating positive symptoms with neuroleptics or behavioral therapies, successful community placement often is limited by the presence of negative symptoms: a lack of social skills or judgment that precludes fully independent living in the community. Successful community placement of such patients requires facilities such as sheltered housing, case management systems, and effective crisis intervention. The state mental health systems that have most successfully deinstitutionalized their younger chronically mentally ill patients are those that have most fully developed and funded these community resources.

In addition to developing community supports, some negative symptoms of chronic mental illness may be amenable to specific social skills training or occupational therapy programs within the state hospital. Because it is often difficult to predict which patients will do well with social skills training alone and which will require long-term community support, it is reasonable to commit some resources to both of these approaches to negative symptoms.

Systems that have effectively developed community resources often are those that pay for hospital and community care out of a common fund, thus creating fiscal incentives for the development of efficient community services. In Rhode Island, for example, community mental health centers are responsible for paying for the state hospital care of all chronically mentally ill individuals in their catchment area. Therefore, every patient they keep out of the state hospital increases funds available for community-based programs. Under this system, state hospital admissions are far less frequent and tend to be shorter than before there were such fiscal incentives.

A striking example of a lack of coordination can also be found in the New England region. In Maine, local communities do not pay for the state hospital care of patients who originate there. Thus the transfer of the patient to the state hospital relieves a locality of the cost of care rather than imposing a cost. Not surprisingly, there are many long-stay patients at the state hospital, and community resources for chronically mentally ill patients are limited. On a recent tour of the Augusta Mental Health Institute, a member of the Task Force found numerous patients in the state hospital, at a daily cost of approximately $300/day, who easily could have been managed in a nursing home with regular consultation from a psychiatrist or a community mental health center. Ironically, this would cost less than state hospital care, even if patients had the finest private rooms at a nursing home in their community and the state paid the full private-pay rate! Such dispositions, however, have not taken place because there are no incentives for them to be made.

Integration of Medical and Psychiatric Care

During the heyday of state hospital care for mentally ill patients, many state hospitals had on-site acute medical hospital beds, and some even had the capacity to perform surgery in keeping with the expectations that residents would remain in the state hospitals for years and with the lack of nonstate funding (i.e., Medicaid) to pay for medical-surgical treatment elsewhere.

The contemporary funding and service environment is different. Between Medicare and Medicaid, most general medical care services for elderly mentally ill patients are fundable largely with federal dollars, as long as the services are rendered in a general medical, rather than a mental, hospital setting. Thus from the funding point of view, it makes sense to provide minimal general medical care within the state hospital and to arrange for most general medical care to be rendered in clinics and hospitals in the general health sector. Clinically, however, this creates problems for effective integration of medical and psychiatric care. Medical specialists in nonpsychiatric facilities may lack experience in examining mentally ill patients for medical problems, and medical care plans recommended by physicians in the general health sector may not be faithfully implemented by psychiatric facilities staff who have had no direct communication with the physician.

Integrating medical and psychiatric care for elderly patients in state mental hospitals challenges administrators to develop creative solutions to capture the fiscal advantages of Medicare and Medicaid funding without losing the benefits of integrated medical and psychiatric care planning. One device deserving consideration is the use of part-time medical consultants who are based at a general health care facility. These consultants could be paid to regularly attend rounds on the psychogeriatric wards to assist in care planning, and to facilitate transfer of patients to inpatient and outpatient general health facilities when more costly and intensive diagnostic or therapeutic interventions are needed. Reciprocal arrangements for state hospital geriatric psychiatrists to consult at neighboring general health facilities could help develop those facilities' abilities to diagnose medical illnesses in the face of acute psychopathology and to manage patients who require inpatient medical care. They might also improve the reputation of the state hospital and its staff among community physicians.

Chapter 5

Alzheimer's Disease and Related Disorders: Responsibilities of State Mental Hospitals

Alzheimer's disease and related disorders (ADRDs) are brain diseases of later life that lead to intellectual impairment, functional incapacitation, and often institutionalization. Before deinstitutionalization, state psychiatric hospitals provided care to large numbers of elderly patients with dementing illnesses (Kobrynski and Miller 1970; Sherwood and Mor 1980; Talbott 1983; Taube et al. 1983). Most of these patients were "transinstitutionalized" to nursing homes, which were considered to be more appropriate settings for the institutional care of ADRD patients (Verwoerdt and Eisdorfer 1967).

Many nursing homes were ill prepared, however, to meet the mental and emotional needs of ADRD patients (Borson et al. 1987). At some point during their course, ADRD patients commonly have mental and behavioral symptoms including depression, paranoia, hallucinations, anxiety, agitation, aggressiveness, and wandering. These concomitants of dementing illness exacerbate disability and challenge caretakers both at home and in institutions. The treatability of these symptoms, however, frequently is not recognized (Butler 1969, 1975; Reisberg et al. 1986). Growing awareness of the limitations of conventional nursing home services has led to the proliferation of Alzheimer Special Care Units (ASCUs) in many nursing homes.

When disruptive behavior exceeds the tolerance of the family or institutional caretakers of an ADRD patient, the state hospital may be considered as an alternative setting of care. Psychiatric hospitalization can be a legitimate intervention for the evaluation and treatment of comorbid psychiatric symptoms in ADRD patients (Group for the Advancement of Psychiatry 1983), and in fact ADRD patients frequently are admitted to private psychiatric facilities or psychiatric units in general hospitals. However, private facilities often have length of stay limits based on Medicare reimbursement limits, and many private facilities do not accept involuntary patients. When involuntary psychiatric hospitalization is necessary, commitment to a state hospital may be warranted. When a short-term private hospital intervention fails, transfer to the state hospital may be rational. And ADRD patients without insurance coverage who require hospitalization may need to seek treatment in the public sector.

In connection with this last point, it should be noted that state hospital care often is available to patients without the proof of impoverishment needed for them to qualify for Medicaid-funded nursing home care. For middle-class families, the out-of-pocket cost of state hospital care, even with the copayments required by some states, may be less than that of private nursing home care.

In 1987, approximately one-third of elderly state hospital patients had ADRD (Moak and Fisher 1990; National Institute of Mental Health, Survey and Reports Branch, Division of Biometry and Applied Sciences 1987). Treatment of ADRD patients—for both short term and long term—remains an important role for state hospitals in most states. However, the appropriate future role for state hospitals in the care of ADRD patients is the subject of controversy. In the remainder of this chapter, we attempt to clarify the issues under dispute. Our discussion leads to the proposal of a core role for state hospitals in the care of ADRD patients. The core is the minimum acceptable role for the state; the ideal for ADRD care is a fully integrated publicly supported care system that not only meets the needs of the most severely impaired and poorest patients, but also addresses the needs of nonindigent patients and families facing earlier or less complicated forms of dementing illness. A universal commitment of state mental health systems to adequate hospital care for those who need it is an important interim goal, because its attainment would put an end to the tragedy of dementia patients with no reasonable place to go.

In the care of patients with dementia, psychiatric inpatient treatment is indicated when behavioral and mental complications such as agitation, psychosis, or depression need treatment or containment that cannot be provided in other environments. Psychiatric hospitalization, because of its expense and its stigma, tends to be a last resort. Its appropriate role varies with what other environments and services are available in the community. A community with specialized psychogeriatric nursing homes or excellent ASCUs has less need for psychiatric hospitalization of persons with dementia than one without such facilities. Similarly, specialized dementia units in nonpsychiatric chronic disease hospitals may provide adequate care to many patients who would otherwise be referred for psychiatric hospitalization.

Within the category of dementia patients needing care for psychiatric hospitalizations, distinctions may be made according to whether 1) hospitalization is voluntary or involuntary, 2) the dementia is mild or severe, or 2) the patient and/or responsible third party can pay for the treatment.

Private sector hospitals currently provide substantial amounts of care to individuals with psychiatric complications of mild dementia who present voluntarily for short-term inpatient treatment covered by Medicare. Many private sector hospitals can even accept involuntary patients for short stays. Some private general hospitals or geriatric hospitals can provide a short-term care for more advanced dementia patients who have substantial cognitive and functional impairment, in addition to behavioral disorder. These facilities often place their discharge patients in nursing homes or accept patients from nursing homes for the purpose of addressing acute behavioral flare-ups.

However, when long-term treatment is needed, few patients can afford care in private facilities because Medicare inpatient psychiatric benefits have a 180-day lifetime limit. Even short-term treatment may not be covered for patients who have had substantial prior treatment that exhausted their lifetime Medicare patient days. Patients who need inpatient treatment and have some combination of involuntary status, lack of funds, and functional impairment tend to become the responsibility of the public sector, which has traditionally attempted to fill the gaps in the United States' health care system. (It did so for tuberculosis in prior decades and now attempts to do so for patients with the human immunodeficiency virus.)

A role for the state, however, does not necessarily imply the use of state mental hospitals. State leadership in organizing and funding the care of these patients could be effected through a range of mechanisms, including contracts with private hospitals, the establishment of specialized psychogeriatric nursing homes, and the creation of specialized public hospital units separate from mental health systems. Each approach has advantages and disadvantages. The huge variance in the rate of state hospital utilization for elderly patients with dementia described in Chapter 1 suggests that the current distribution of dementia patients among various care providers strongly reflects local resources and traditions and that the future role of the state hospital in the care of dementia patients may continue to be more locality specific. In all states, rational discussion of policy options and unmet needs is required.

A rational policy discussion within any particular state might begin with an assessment of available resources, asking questions such as how often private psychiatric hospitals take involuntary patients, whether general hospitals have special units for the care of physically frail elderly patients with combined medical and psychiatric disorders, and whether there are public chronic disease hospitals with current or potential dementia care capacities. Areas of unmet need would then be analyzed, and efforts would be made to determine where appropriate new capacity could be added at the lowest marginal cost. In some states, it might be appropriate to add a psychiatric consultation-liaison service and additional psychiatric nurses to existing chronic disease hospitals. In other states, the physical plant, staff, and administration of chronic disease hospitals might not be amenable to this option, and upgrading the general medical and rehabilitative capacities of units in state psychiatric hospitals might be more cost-effective. In this ideal situation, the ultimate decisions would depend on a rational needs assessment and cost analysis. In practice, however, other concerns may take precedence and lead to a more adversarial tone in discussions on the locus of dementia care. These concerns are those of 1) stigma, 2) competition within agencies for limited resources, and 3) cost-shifting agendas of states and the federal government.

Stigma

Mental illness is stigmatized; brain disease is not. For this reason, the Alzheimer's Disease and Related Disorders Association has emphasized its view that Alzheimer's disease is *not* a mental illness, and the National

Alliance for the Mentally Ill (NAMI) has emphasized that schizophrenia and manic-depressive illness *are* brain diseases. Patients with brain diseases, including dementia, may behave in ways intolerable to society in general, leading to a demand for institutional care. Mental hospitals historically have been the locus of care for persons with unacceptable behavior. However, admission to a mental hospital implies stigma, even if the reason is a brain disease. Advocates for persons with dementia appear to want two things: nonstigmatized facilities for the care of dementia patients with socially unacceptable behavior and the same entitlement to care from the state that is currently available for mentally ill patients, including the option of protective involuntary treatment at state expense. The establishment of special units or hospitals for dementia patients not under state mental health authorities might meet these needs, but the development of an entirely new system of care would be most difficult at a time when states are attempting to restrain their fiscal commitments.

Competition Within Agencies for Resources

The reluctance of many state mental health authorities to assume additional responsibility for dementia care derives from the concern that this incremental burden would not be covered by commensurate new fiscal resources from the state treasury. State mental health planners fear that dementia care would come at the expense of other important and underfunded groups, such as young chronically mentally ill and homeless mentally ill populations.

The increase in elderly individuals at risk for dementia aggravates this problem. The assumption by the states of a more primary role in dementia care implies the assumption of an ever-increasing burden. Even the appropriation of categorical funds for dementia care, not in competition with other state mental health programs, may not be a solution. Because entire mental health budgets tend to be viewed as a unit by policy makers and the public, state mental health authority responsibility for the bulk of dementia care could ultimately lead to a political attack on the "explosive growth of state mental health budgets." Advocates for younger mentally ill patients, such as NAMI, fear that programs for younger mental patients would be likely to suffer their share of the inevitable budget cuts.

In the long term, a greater role for state government in funding and coordinating dementia care is appropriate. Development of such a role requires interagency cooperation between departments of health, mental health, housing, and human services to build a true continuum of care. It also requires political consensus among advocates for dementia patients and advocates for chronically mentally ill patients, so that political pressure is aimed at a general increase in needed services, rather than at diversion of resources from one group in need to another.

Cost-Shifting Agendas

A central political issue in the United States has been the division and responsibility between the states and the federal government for various social services. Explosive growth of Medicaid expenditures has been in part the consequence of states shifting to the federal government (which partially funds Medicaid) the cost of caring for indigent patients who were formerly the responsibility of state public hospitals and mental hospitals. An important example is the shifting of mentally ill elderly patients to nursing homes and, in some states, to nonpsychiatric chronic disease hospitals, both of which are eligible to receive Medicaid payments as long as they are not "institutions for mental diseases." The latter are defined as facilities in which more than half of the residents have mental illness diagnoses.

The definition of *ADRD* as "not mental illness" is necessary to preserve the federal role in funding dementia care by Medicaid. This having been accomplished by legislation, it is understandable that state authorities would choose to provide the vast bulk of dementia care in nursing homes and chronic hospitals that are eligible for Medicaid, rather than in state psychiatric hospitals not eligible for Medicaid. Every dementia patient treated in a Medicaid-eligible facility represents substantial costs shifted from the state budget to the federal budget.

Current State Initiatives

The National Association of State Mental Health Program Directors (NASMHPD) unanimously adopted a resolution on 13 December 1989 opposing federal targeting or mandating state mental health agency responsibilities or funds for specific disease populations, such as individuals with ADRDs and individuals with acquired immunodeficiency syndrome (AIDS). The resolution acknowledged that many state mental health authorities already serve such persons in many ways and encouraged state initiatives to meet the mental health needs of these special populations, as resources permitted.

According to the *1990 Alzheimer's Association Directory of State Alzheimer's Programs and Legislation* (Alzheimer's Association 1990), state mental health agencies currently have specific statutory and/or program responsibility for persons with Alzheimer's disease in eight states: California, Florida, Maryland, Michigan, Oregon, South Carolina, Virginia, and Washington. Authority is statutory in California and Florida; programmatic only in Maryland, Oregon, South Carolina, and Washington; and both statutory and programmatic in Michigan and Virginia. In all of these states, responsibility for patients with Alzheimer's disease is shared with other state agencies, including departments of aging, health, and human services. Specific responsibilities assumed by the state mental health agencies include inpatient services for patients with psychosis and severe behavioral management problems.

In three of the six states in which there is programmatic responsibility for the state mental health agency for Alzheimer's disease patients, there is a line item in the state mental health authority budget for the care of individuals with Alzheimer's disease. In all other states, funds spent by state mental health authorities on Alzheimer patients are commingled with the general budget. In a 1989 survey of state mental health agencies conducted by NASMHPD, 20 of 31 states reporting indicated that the state mental health agency spent some of its funds on patients with Alzheimer's disease. The amounts were substantial: well over $2 million a year in Illinois and New Jersey, two states in which there is no specific statutory or program responsibility of the state mental health agency for Alzheimer's disease patients. Not surprisingly, the overwhelming majority of state program directors responding to the NASMHPD survey indicated that they would oppose a federal mandate for state mental health agency involvement in Alzheimer's disease care.

In 1989 the National Conference of State Legislatures (NCSL) stated its official policy on ADRDs. In its official statement, it recognized the importance of providing a continuum of care, ranging from home care to community-based care to institutional care, and emphasized the role of the federal government in Alzheimer's disease research and in developing new funding mechanisms for formal long-term care. NCSL supported policy that would assure Alzheimer's disease patients and their families access to mental health services. However, NCSL strongly stated that it did not believe that ADRDs should be solely a state responsibility and that it opposed mandates or initiatives to establish it as such.

In April 1990, NASMHPD recommended a number of technical amendments to the Medicaid program related to the role of state mental health agencies in the care of medically ill elderly patients. Among the amendments were efforts to 1) restrict the scope of preadmission screening and annual resident review (PASARR), thereby reducing the number of nursing home patients the state mental health agency would be obliged to screen; 2) restrict the definition of *active treatment* in the PASARR provision to reduce the number of patients to whom it would apply; 3) restrict the definition of *institutions for mental diseases (IMDs)* to allow nursing homes to address their residents' mental health problems without being reclassified as an IMD; and 4) permit nursing homes under the auspices of state mental health agencies not to be automatically classified as IMDs because of their sponsorship. All of these recommended technical amendments go in the direction of limiting state mental health agencies' *obligations* to provide and finance care for elderly persons with a combination of medical illness, dementia, and behavioral symptoms. The state mental health agencies recognize a primary and historical role in caring for patients with primary and major mental illnesses. For the most part, they do not regard the mental problems of dementia patients as necessarily their responsibility. Further, they regard it as appropriate to transfer patients from state mental hospitals to Medicaid-funded long-term care facilities should the patients' physical frailty and/or dementia outweigh the severity of their active mental problems.

In *State Issues 1990* (National Conference of State Legislature, 1990), a report of the survey of 1,500 state legislators and legislative staff, NCSL reported on the priority of elderly issues. The two top concerns of the state legislators and their staffs were alternatives to institutional care and access and funding of long-term care. Specialty care, including both Alzheimer's disease care and mental health care were significantly lower on the list.[1] This suggests that a positive strategy for state mental health agencies in the current environment is to promote the development of community-based resources, both institutional and noninstitutional, for care of dementia patients or mentally ill elderly patients. These resources are likely to obtain more legislative support and additional funds for state hospitals themselves. Success in developing community alternatives may permit further reduction in the numbers of elderly residents of state hospitals, without compromising quality of care.

Implications for the Core State Hospital Role

These considerations argue for a restricted role of state mental hospitals in the care of dementia patients. We submit that the following be considered the "core" role of state mental hospitals in dementia care. A greater or lesser role for the state hospitals would be appropriate according to states' other resources and historical commitments.

1. Short-term involuntary treatment (diagnosis, stabilization, and disposition) for dementia patients who pose an acute danger to themselves or others, or who face criminal charges for dementia-related behavior
2. Short-term treatment to assess and stabilize violent behavior in nursing home patients, when suitable alternatives for such service do not exist in psychiatric nursing homes or private sector hospital services.
3. Long-term care of dementia patients with chronic behavioral symptoms unmanageable in nursing homes and not responsive to acute treatment.
4. Care of patients with a combination of dementia and chronic primary mental illness, where the latter would in itself indicate chronic placement in a state psychiatric hospital.

---

[1] The fact that Alzheimer's disease made the list at all is nonetheless remarkable, as the disease was virtually unknown to the general public two decades ago.

Chapter 6

The State Hospital as a Site for Training in Geriatric Psychiatry

Traditionally, training sites for geriatric psychiatry fellowship programs have been located in university medical centers, community mental health facilities, Veterans Administration hospitals, and nursing homes (Gaitz et al. 1981; Jacobson and Juthani 1978). State hospitals deserve a place on this list.

State hospital populations comprise a variety of chronic and treatment-refractory patients and are usually poorly staffed by psychiatrists. This gives fellows exposure to a wide range of severe and chronic psychopathology, in a setting that permits them to make a real and meaningful contribution to patient care. Also the state hospital setting, with a proper academic liaison, can offer invaluable experiences in administration and management and in the practical application of clinical and health services research and evaluation techniques. Training programs that successfully link university medical centers with state hospital systems offer the possibility of true synergy. The payment of a fellow's salary is a relatively small item in a state hospital budget, whereas the quality and amount of service delivered by a motivated and well-supervised fellow is a bargain for the amount spent. On the other hand, hard dollars from a state hospital salary line may be extremely attractive to a financially pressed academic department, and the liaison with the public sector may open new possibilities for recruiting research subjects or facilitate competition for certain research grants.

The training of fellows can be part of a more extensive state hospital–university medical center liaison that offers advantages for training residents in the care of chronically mentally ill patients. In one innovative program at the University of Massachusetts, state hospital populations have been used to train psychiatry residents in neurology. The patients at the state hospital have a high prevalence of neurological disorders, including dementia, and the psychiatry residents' evaluations of these patients under neurologists' supervision offers them neurological experience possibly more relevant than that obtainable in a typical general neurology clinic.

The Medical College of Virginia has had a particularly positive experience with the state hospital as a training site for fellows in geriatric psychiatry. That experience is published in detail elsewhere (Colenda et al. 1991). The Medical College of Virginia experience has highlighted three training objectives particularly relevant for geriatric psychiatrists that may be readily accomplished by rotations at a state hospital. These are 1) training in administration and management, 2) acquisition of skills as an educator of professional and support staff, and 3) development of applied clinical research skills, particularly in the areas of outcome measurement, program evaluation, and translating research findings into clinical practice.

A. Development of Administrative and Management Skills

Physicians often have had minimal exposure to principles and strategies of management and to the ideas of organizational analysis. Because improved psychogeriatric services depend on the leadership of geriatric psychiatrists, management training for geriatric psychiatrists is essential so that they can act as effective partners with the usually nonmedical administrators who run state mental health systems. Training in four core areas of management is necessary: personnel management, organizational and departmental relations, program development, and budgeting.

Personnel management. In long-term care facilities, personnel management cannot easily be ignored, yet some physicians show distaste or indifference to the task of supervising professional personnel and support staff. Positive attitudes toward personnel management can be developed by training psychiatrists in techniques of performance assessment. Through on-site experience in personnel evaluation under the supervision of senior administrators, fellows can learn how to establish and measure performance criteria for employees.

Another management skill that can be acquired through supervised experience is conflict resolution. As in other administrative assignments such as chief residencies, geriatric fellows in the state hospital can learn how to make use of their specialized knowledge of personal relations to solve problems, without inappropriately assuming the role of a group psychotherapist.

Organizational and departmental relations.   During their careers, geriatric psychiatrists will deal with numerous agencies and organizations, each involved with some aspect of the care of elderly or mentally ill patients. Supervised experience, particularly in placing patients in the community and in organizing aftercare, can enhance fellows' appreciation of these issues. The state hospital experience also gives fellows a thorough understanding of the strengths and limitations of the state hospital as a source of care for mentally ill elderly patients.

Program development.   Because all state hospital psychogeriatric services have clinical and administrative problems to solve, a fellowship can offer the fellow an opportunity to develop a solution to a specific clinical, educational, or administrative problem. The fellow chooses an area of clinical need, formulates a small-scale program solution, develops a budget, and carries out the program during the fellowship year. At the Medical College of Virginia program, most fellows chose to develop educational programs to improve diagnostic and clinical skills of specific hospital personnel. Other options for fellows' projects include developing or expanding aftercare programs for specific groups of patients or doing liaison work with rest homes, nursing homes, or family practice organizations in the region.

Budgeting.   Future role expectations for institutionally based geriatric psychiatrists are likely to include not only program development, but also fiscal management. Many general psychiatry residents have little understanding of how to make realistic budgets and keep projects within them. The state hospital offers an ideal setting for learning about routine budget planning, Medicare and Medicaid programs, the financing of long-term care, division of responsibility among payers, and managing the sort of budgetary crises that regularly arise in the public sector. Both faculty psychiatrists and state hospital administrators can function as teachers for the fellows in this context. In some state systems, state hospital administrators are given clinical faculty appointments at the medical school in recognition of this activity.

B. Development of the Geriatric Psychiatrist as Educator

Because of their diversity of staff and their challenging patient populations, state hospitals offer excellent opportunities for geriatric psychiatry fellows to develop skills in staff education. Because of their recent and contemporary experience, geriatric psychiatry fellows can be particularly sought-after sources of information for nonmedical health care professionals, support staff, and family caretakers.

The staff of state hospital psychogeriatric services offer a population of learners eager to gain more knowledge of diagnosis and treatment, who are less likely than their counterparts in academic medical centers to be overloaded with various learning opportunities. Their questions to the geriatric psychiatry fellows also represent the learning needs that the fellow is likely to encounter in liaison work throughout his or her career. If the fellows' experiences as educators are supervised by faculty who are themselves good teachers, their strengths as educators can be developed and their weaknesses addressed.

C. Development of Research and Evaluation Skills

Conducting research is not the major professional activity of most geriatric psychiatrists. However, the interpretation of research findings and their translation into clinical practice are necessary skills for all practitioners of this new psychiatric specialty. Assessing new research and bringing it into clinical application is especially pertinent in state hospitals, where research advances are often slow to be incorporated into clinical practice.

At the Medical College of Virginia program, research training was designed to enhance the fellow's capacity as a *prudent consumer* of research reports. The training was flexible and attempted to match the training needs and professional interests of the fellow with the research needs of the university and the state hospital. Research training for the fellow represents a combination of didactic sessions on the basics of experimental design, measurement, and biostatistics, followed by a supervised experience in small-scale clinical research. The major skills to be acquired through this small-scale research experience are 1) formulating a research question in response to a clinical or administrative problem, 2) selecting appropriate subject samples and measurement tools, 3) analyzing the data, and 4) choosing appropriate statistical tests for the significance of results. The skills are focused in the area of applied research, with an emphasis on needs assessment, program evaluation, and outcome assessment studies. These types of research are perhaps the most likely to be carried out by a geriatric psychiatrist outside of an academic setting.

Fellowship training programs associated with medical schools with academic strengths in health services research or outcomes research could offer fellows the opportunity to participate in more ambitious projects involving measurement of the quality and outcomes of care. Fellowships affiliated with departments active in geriatric psychopharmacology research could involve fellows in controlled trials of drug treatment for common late-life mental disorders.

Chapter 7

Recommendations for Action

In the preceding chapters, we have attempted to show that state mental hospitals currently play a significant role in the care of mentally ill elderly patients and suggested that they will continue in a reduced but still-important role even when trends toward deinstitutionalization and trans-institutionalization have reached their limit. We have also advanced an ideal of quality and offered the hope that a public sector–academic liaison would be a small step toward that ideal. In this concluding chapter, we consider how state hospitals might improve their quality of care and help develop a fuller continuum of care, despite constraints of tight budgets and bureaucratic traditions. We offer a number of options for consideration, aware that each may be more or less applicable within a given state or hospital system. They are grouped according to general categories: 1) clarifying goals and objectives, 2) recruiting and developing personnel, 3) integrating psychiatric with general geriatric medical care, 4) improving administrative conditions for quality care, and 5) employing outcome-based quality assurance strategies.

1. Clarifying Goals and Objectives

Clear goals and objectives facilitate quality and efficiency at all levels, from the level of the state mental health program director down to the individual clinical units. At the state level, program directors should, in collaboration with those of other state agencies, define that portion of geriatric care that is their responsibility. For example, which patients with dementia belong in state mental hospitals and which should be cared for elsewhere? If the state hospital is to have a gap-filling function, efforts should be made to explicitly determine what gaps are to be filled. The analyses of Chapters 4 and 5 of this report might be applicable to the task of defining the state system's role.

At the hospital level, the superintendent and medical director should delineate the institution's clinical goals and its goals for relation to the community and to other providers of care. Is the hospital's main goal to provide long-term custodial care or to provide rapid diagnosis and stabilization? Or, is it to do both, for different populations? Will the hospital assume general geriatric medical care responsibilities, or will there be a low threshold for transferring any patients who become acutely ill to general medical facilities? Will screening of hospital admissions be carried out by community mental health centers (CMHCs)? Will all patients referred from the community for admission actually be admitted?

At the level of the ward or treatment unit, clinical leadership must similarly identify goals. For example, does the unit leadership set the goal of a community placement for all patients, unless repeated past attempts to make such placements have failed? Does the unit have the goal of independently reevaluating and confirming old diagnoses of schizophrenia? Does it have the goal of diagnosing and attempting to address impairments of gait and mobility, or is this seen as the function of some other provider of care?

In Chapter 3, we presented a highly ambitious set of goals for a state hospital psychogeriatric service. It is doubtful if the complete set is attainable in any state system, but it is likely that several of the suggested goals would be attainable on almost any unit. The choice of a set of specific and attainable goals may improve the likelihood that goals will be reached and may help to improve staff morale because a game is defined that it is possible to win.

Different treatment goals may be appropriate for different units. A strong case could be made that at least one clinical unit in each institution should be dedicated to the acute, aggressive treatment of recently admitted patients with either acute or relapsing disorders, where substantial improvement and discharge to the community is the likely result of an aggressive approach. Concentrating patients with an acute illness and a good prognosis on a specific unit might improve their outcome by creating a more hopeful and optimistic milieu. On the other hand, wards with more chronically and severely impaired individuals might adopt realistic goals for modest improvements in function, comfort, or autonomy that would be specific and attainable and counter tendencies toward a purely custodial approach.

2. Recruiting and Developing Personnel

There can be little argument that adequate numbers of well-trained and enthusiastic psychiatrists and general physicians are needed for a state hospital to offer outstanding care. Many state systems do not offer salaries compatible with private practice, but whether or not they do, qualitative aspects of the psychiatrist's job may be of greater importance than pay in recruiting and retaining high-quality medical staff. A number of specific programs might make state hospitals more appealing work sites for excellent psychiatrists and general physicians:

a. Link state hospitals to academic medical centers, so that staff physicians can more easily get continuing medical education and case-specific subspecialist consultation. Clinical faculty appointments and teaching opportunities could also be offered when appropriate. With a strong public-academic liaison, fellows and residents can become involved in patient care at the state hospital, thereby increasing the physician pool and continually exposing the permanent staff to new ideas and approaches (Weintraub et al. 1984).

b. Offer greater autonomy to psychiatrists with leadership abilities and facilitate their collaboration with administrators and nonmedical professionals in running the hospital and its units. Some degree of direct budgetary control enhances the job satisfaction of unit chiefs and medical directors and fosters their creativity. Major involvement of psychiatrists in the selection, training, and evaluation of nonmedical staff and in the development and implementation of quality assurance programs also has the potential for improving their morale and their effectiveness. (Reciprocally, leaders of the nonmedical professional disciplines should participate in the selection, training, and evaluation of the medical staff: the issue is physician empowerment, not physician domination.)

c. Offer staff psychiatrists training and continuing education in the administrative and managerial components of their work. Many excellent clinicians lack a detailed understanding of financial, legal, and management issues relevant to public sector psychiatric practice. Lacking this understanding, they become frustrated by the environment of the state hospital. With an understanding, they may be more able to bear the frustrations of the system and more able to contribute creative solutions to institutional problems. Training should address the personal and professional issues involved in working for bosses who are not physicians.

d. Create opportunities for part-time involvement by community-based and academic psychiatrists. Many psychiatrists would find work with the state hospital psychogeriatric population challenging and interesting, but would not choose to do it full time. Part-time work, suitably organized and compensated, might be attractive to a number of excellent people. Their knowledge and skills would enrich the permanent full-time staff.

e. Recruit recently trained geriatricians to coordinate the general medical care of the patients. Thousands of geriatric specialists have been trained in recent years in a holistic and comprehensive model of care of frail elderly patients. Such people should be vigorously recruited for both full-time and part-time positions.

f. Contract with specialists in behavioral neurology, neuropsychology, and neuropsychiatry to assist with difficult diagnostic problems. Although few such specialists would work full-time at a state mental hospital, many would be fascinated by the patient population and would be attracted to adequately paid part-time or consulting work. Their input could be expected not only to improve the quality of care of individual patients, but to raise the level of diagnostic sophistication of the entire staff.

g. Make use of nurse practitioners and physicians' assistants to make the work of the geriatricians and general medical physicians more interesting and less routine. Recruitment and improvement of nonmedical staff is equally important and could be facilitated by many of the same general strategies.

h. Recruit nonmedical professionals with specialized training in geriatrics and gerontology. Schools of psychology, nursing, social work, and occupational therapy offer specialized gerontological curricula. Their graduates might be attracted to state hospital work, if offered inducements such as a pay differential, a role in teaching gerontology to other staff, some autonomy and budgetary control, and the option of part-time or flexible-hours work. The visible presence of physicians who understand and value the contribution of nonmedical professionals and can gracefully share authority with them might also attract specialists of the nonmedical professions.

i. Provide continuing education to all staff, from attendants on up. Continuing education on both psychiatric and medical topics is particularly important for lower-status staff, for whom ongoing education, training, and supervision may enhance morale and self-esteem, as well as provide substantive knowledge and skills.

3. Integrating Psychiatric With General Geriatric Care

Because of the high prevalence of comorbid physical illness in the state hospital population, integration of psychiatric and medical care is crucial to care quality. As noted in Chapter 2, recent litigation on behalf of patients claiming injury while in state hospitals specifically addressed the poor quality of medical care received by some of the patients.

Integration of psychiatric and medical care is also a potential source of cost savings to state mental health authorities, because it is sometimes possible to shift medical care costs from the state hospital to Medicare or Medicaid by having patients get needed medical diagnostic or treatment procedures outside the state hospital, either at a private physician's office or at a general hospital or clinic. Such cost offsets should be pursued whenever possible, applying the money saved to pay for greater involvement of geriatricians and other medical specialists in treatment planning.

Integration of medical and psychiatric care often facilitates earlier discharge or transfer of a patient from the state hospital. Sometimes, correction of medical problems permits sufficient recovery of function for the patient to be discharged to the community. On the other hand, careful diagnostic assessment sometimes uncovers permanent and irreversible functional deficits with a medical etiology that might be the basis of an appropriate transfer to a nursing home.

An important aspect of any medical and psychiatric care is recognizing and minimizing adverse interactions between treatments for medical and psychiatric conditions. These effects operate in both directions: methyldopa prescribed for hypertension may aggravate depression; lithium-induced polyuria may aggravate incontinence. We recommend

a. An experienced general internist or geriatrician should participate in psychogeriatric treatment planning meetings.
b. Efforts should be made to arrange for general medical care of state hospital patients in settings where Medicare or Medicaid will pay, to remove financial disincentives for treatment.
c. Continuing education for medical and nonmedical staff alike should include coverage of common geriatric problems such as incontinence, gait disturbance, and delirium.
d. Psychogeriatric emergency services should be either located in general hospitals or clinically and administratively linked to emergency medical services at general hospitals. Rapid medical assessment should be facilitated for elderly patients who present with behavioral crises. Likewise, psychiatric assessment and liaison should be available for patients who present to emergency services with a combination of urgent medical illness and uncooperative behavior.

4. Improving Administrative Conditions for Quality Care

Analysts of mental health policy recurrently identify problems due to "perverse incentives" and cost shifting. The former problem is exemplified by insurance that fully covers inpatient care but has no outpatient coverage, thus favoring hospitalization when less costly outpatient treatment would be effective. The latter is exemplified by the transinstitutionalization of patients from state hospitals to nursing homes because the latter are covered by Medicaid. There is widespread consensus that the elimination of these problems would improve the quality of care and facilitate the development of the continuum of services. Common recommendations argue for the pooling of resources for the care of a defined at-risk population, combining monies from Medicare, Medicaid, localities, and sometimes the individuals themselves. Case management is then employed to allocate services to clients. Well-known demonstration programs, such as On Lok in San Francisco, have shown this to be an effective strategy for managing care of frail community-dwelling elderly individuals. However, specific trials for chronically mentally ill elderly patients have not been conducted.

Partial efforts to resolve these problems at the state level are typified by the Rhode Island model, in which CMHCs in effect must pay their clients' hospital bills out of their total annual budgets. Thus the dollar in hospital costs saved is a dollar available to be spent on community support services. The Task Force favors approaches that support a full continuum of care and create incentives for the development of community resources. Some examples include

a. At the state level, resources for chronically mentally ill elderly patients should be pooled by region or locality and should be used to develop a continuum of care. The total pool might be a line item in the state budget, linked to the number of elders at risk by a reasonable capitation formula. CMHCs should have direct or indirect incentives to develop or purchase community services for their elderly clients and should use the state hospital only for a relatively narrow range of specific indications as discussed in Chapters 4 and 5. States should take the option of providing case management benefits for elderly chronically mentally ill patients covered by Medicaid.

b. At the hospital level, individual unit chiefs should have incentives for making successful dispositions of patients to the community. This might take the form of funds or other resources that would be available contingent on meeting a target rate of successful dispositions over a defined time period. Resources could then be used by the unit chief to develop community resources, to address community liaison needs, or to develop programs and staff of the unit itself.

c. Unit chiefs should have the flexibility to facilitate placements by offering extra support to the receiving facility or agency. For example, a unit chief should be able to offer a nursing home follow-up consultation on behavioral management or guarantee that the patient would be readmitted if he or she proved unmanageable even with consultation. Such flexibility is tantamount to the hospital director offering a discretionary budget to unit chiefs for the purpose of making more community dispositions.

5. Emphasizing Outcome-Based Quality Assurance Strategies

Efforts to measure medical care quality while measuring outcomes of care represent the leading edge of quality assurance technology. Outcome-based quality assurance, properly done, lacks the potentially alienating quality of rigid externally imposed standards. The measurement and dissemination of clinically meaningful outcome measures enables clinical staff to strive for continual improvement, to be recognized for their successes, and to promote innovative strategies to make outcomes better.

The technology of outcome-based quality assurance is relatively new, and it is not always clear what to measure or how to measure it. Nonetheless, geriatric psychiatry units in state hospitals can begin by measuring some outcomes with face validity and with well-established measures. These include the average length of stay of residents, according to diagnosis; the proportion of patients successfully placed in the community over a given time; and the proportion of patients who improve in functional independence over a fixed period. Standard psychiatric rating scales such as the Hamilton Depression Rating Scale and the Brief Psychiatric Rating Scale can also be used for measuring improvement in specific clinical syndromes.

The widespread employment of systematic outcome assessment and feedback to staff of outcome data, used as a tool for continuous quality improvement, is best envisioned as separate from arbitrary and external standards for the outcomes themselves. Units are likely to begin with different outcomes because of differences in patient population, staffing, and resource endowment. However, all of them can aim for continual improvement, and positive reinforcement of staff for better outcomes is one way to bring this about.

Systematic outcome measurement would also permit systems to identify units that obtain particularly good results for specific clinical problems. A study of their organizational structures, treatment programs, or staff training methods might identify techniques and programs that can be transferred to other units in the state's system.

Systematic outcome assessment feedback and incentives for improvement work against rigid institutional traditions. Indirectly, this may aid in the recruitment, retention, and development of highly skilled personnel. The choice of outcomes to be measured obviously is linked to the goals and objectives of the unit and the institution. The use of measures for medical, cognitive, and functional outcomes, as well as for psychiatric outcomes, facilitates the integration of medical and psychiatric care. Changes in rules and administrative policies can be evaluated in part by how well they facilitate improvement in outcomes.

Conclusions

State mental hospitals often have the unglamorous role of the gap filler and the last resort for mentally ill elderly patients. Nonetheless, this role played with enthusiasm and creativity may be invaluable for patients and their families and rewarding for the staff whose hard work makes it possible.

References

Ahr PR, Holcomb WR: State mental health directors' priorities for mental health care. Hosp Community Psychiatry 36:39–45, 1985

Alzheimer's Association: 1990 Alzheimer's Association Directory of State Alzheimer Programs and Legislation. Chicago, IL, Alzheimer's Association, 1990

Barton WE: The place, if any, of the mental hospital in the community mental health care system. Psychiatr Q 55:146–155, 1983

Borson S, Liptzin B, Nininger J, et al: Psychiatry and the nursing home. Am J Psychiatry 144:1412–1418, 1987

Buchanan AE, Brock DW: Deciding for Others: The Ethics of Surrogate Decision Making. Cambridge, England, Cambridge University Press, 1989

Burns BJ, Taube CA: Mental health services in general medical care and in nursing homes, in Mental Health Policy for Older Americans: Protecting Minds at Risk. Edited by Fogel BS, Furino A, Gottlieb GL. Washington, DC, American Psychiatric Press, 1990, pp 63–84

Butler RN: Ageism: another form of bigotry. Gerontologist 9:243–246, 1969

Butler RN: Psychiatry and the elderly: an overview. Am J Psychiatry 132:893–900, 1975

Checker A: Capital projects funding for psychiatric hospitals, 1972–81. Hosp Community Psychiatry 37:380–385, 1986

Colenda CC: The psychiatry chief resident as information manager. Journal of Medical Education 61:666–673, 1986

Colenda CC, Dougherty L, Lewis R, et al: State-university training in geriatric psychiatry. Hosp Community Psychiatry 42:462–464, 1991

Dawkins J, Depp FC, Selzer N: Occupational stress in a public mental hospital: the psychiatrist view. Hosp Community Psychiatry 35:56–60, 1984

Department of Health and Human Services: Health U.S.A., 1985. Rockville, MD, U.S. Department of Health and Human Services, Public Health Service, 1985, p 103 (table 59)

Dittmar ND, Franklin JL: State hospital patients discharged to nursing homes: are hospitals dumping their more difficult patients? Hosp Community Psychiatry 31:251–254, 1980

Epstein LJ: The elderly mentally ill: finding the right treatment. Hosp Community Psychiatry 26:303–305, 1975

Fink A, Siu AL, Brook RH, et al: Assuring the quality of health care for older persons: an expert panel's priorities. JAMA 258:1905–1908, 1987

Flemming AS, Rickards LD, Santos JF, et al: Mental Health Services for the Elderly: Report on a Survey of Community Mental Health Centers, Vol 3. Washington, DC, Action Committee to Implement the Mental Health Recommendations of the 1981 White House Conference on Aging, 1986

Ford CV, Sbordone RJ: Attitudes of psychiatrists towards elderly patients. Am J Psychiatry 137:571–575, 1980

Gaitz CM: Barriers to the delivery of psychiatric services to the elderly. Gerontologist 14:210–214, 1974

Gaitz CM, Varner RV, Niederehe G: Clinical fellowship program in geriatric psychiatry and psychology. Gerontology and Geriatrics Education 1:181–184, 1981

Galasso D: Guidelines for developing multidisciplinary treatment plans. Hosp Community Psychiatry 38:394–397, 1987

Governor's Task Force on Alzheimer's Disease and Related Disorders: The Maryland Report on Alzheimer's Disease and Related Disorders. Annapolis, MD, State of Maryland, 1985

Greene S, Witkin MJ, Atay J, et al: State and County Mental Hospitals, United States, 1982–83 and 1983–84 with Trend Analysis from 1973–74 to 1983–84 (Statistical Note #176). Rockville, MD, U.S. Department of Health and Human Services, National Institute of Mental Health, 1986

Group for the Advancement of Psychiatry: Mental Health and Aging: Approaches to Curriculum Development (Publication 114). New York, Mental Health Materials Center, 1983

Jacobson SB, Juthani N: The nursing home and training in geropsychiatry. J Am Geriatr Soc 26:408–410, 1978

Kahn RL: The mental health system and the future aged. Gerontologist 15 (suppl):24–31, 1975

Kobrynski B, Miller AD: The role of the state hospital in the care of the elderly. J Am Geriatr Soc 18:210–219, 1970

Lazarus LW, Weinberg J: Training in geropsychiatry: problems and process. Am J Psychiatry 138:1366–1369, 1981

Massachusetts Department of Health: Policy on Admissions Criteria to DMH Inpatient Facilities (Policy #88-4). Boston, MA, Department of Mental Health, 1988

McCarrick AK, Rosenstein MJ, Milazzo-Sayre LJ, et al: National trends in use of psychotherapy in psychiatric inpatient settings. Hosp Community Psychiatry 39:835–841, 1988

Menninger WW: Dealing with staff reactions to perceived lack of progress by chronic mental patients. Hosp Community Psychiatry 35:805–808, 1984

Milazzo-Sayre LJ, Benson PR, Rosenstein MJ, et al: Use of inpatient psychiatric services by the elderly age 65 and over: United States, 1980 (Mental Health Statistical Note No 181). Bethesda, MD, National Institute of Mental Health, Division of Biometry and Applied Sciences, 1987

Miller RD: Public mental hospital work: pros and cons for psychiatrist. Hosp Community Psychiatry 35:928–933, 1984

Moak GS: Treating elderly chronic patients in state hospitals. Hosp Community Psychiatry 39:119–120, 124, 1988

Moak GS, Fisher WH: Alzheimer's disease and related disorders in state mental hospitals: data from a nationwide survey. Gerontologist 30:798–802, 1990

Molnar G, Fava GA: Intercurrent medical illness in the schizophrenic patient, in Principles of Medical Psychiatry. Edited by Stoudemire A, Fogel BS. Orlando, FL, Grune & Stratton, 1987, pp 451–462

Morris JN, Hawes C, Fries BE, et al: Designing the National Resident Assessment Instrument for Nursing Homes. Gerontologist 30:293–307, 1990

National Association of State Mental Health Program Directors Study #89-650: Level II 43 SMHAs Release 1989 OBRA NF Level II Implementation Experiences in Preadmission Screening for Mental Illness. OBRA NF Bulletin #33-III, September 21, 1990

National Conference of State Legislature: State Issues 1990. Washington, DC, National Conference of State Legislatures, 1990

National Institute of Mental Health, Survey and Reports Branch, Division of Biometry and Applied Sciences: Additions and resident patients at end of year state and county mental hospitals, by age and diagnosis, by state, United States. Rockville, MD, National Institute of Mental Health, 1972, 1977, 1982, 1987

PDR Drug Interactions and Side Effects System. Oradell, NJ, Medical Economics, 1989

Reisberg B, Borenstein J, Franssen E, et al: Remediable behavioral symptomatology in Alzheimer's disease. Hosp Community Psychiatry 37:1199–1201, 1986

Robinson GK: The psychiatric component of long-term care models, in Mental Health Policy for Older Americans: Protecting Minds at Risk. Edited by Fogel BS, Furino A, Gottlieb GL. Washington, DC, American Psychiatric Press, 1990, pp 157–177

Sharfstein SS: Payment for services: a provider's perspective, in Mental Health Policy for Older Americans: Protecting Minds at Risk. Edited by Fogel BS, Furino A, Gottlieb GL. Washington, DC, American Psychiatric Press, 1990, pp 97–107

Sherwood S, Mor V: Mental health institutions and the elderly, in Handbook of Mental Health and Aging. Edited by Birren JE, Sloane RB. Englewood Cliffs, NJ, Prentice-Hall, 1980, pp 854–884

Swan JH: The substitution of nursing home for inpatient psychiatric care. Community Ment Health J 23:3–18, 1987

Talbott JA: The Death of the Asylum. New York, Grune & Stratton, 1978

Talbott JA: A special population: the elderly deinstitutionalized chronically mentally ill. Psychiatr Q 55:90–105, 27, 1983

Taube CA, Thompson JW, Rosenstein MJ, et al: The "chronic" mental hospital patient. Hosp Community Psychiatry 34:611–615, 1983

Verwoerdt A, Eisdorfer C: Geropsychiatry: the psychiatry of senescence. Geriatrics 22:139–149, 1967

Waxman HM: Community mental health care for the elderly: a look at the obstacles. Public Health Rep 101:294–300, 1986

Waxman HM, Carver EA: Physicians' recognition, diagnosis and treatment of psychiatric disorders in elderly medical patients. Gerontologist 24:503–509, 1984

Weintraub W, Harbin HT, Book J, et al: The Maryland Plan for recruiting psychiatrists into public service. Am J Psychiatry 141:91–94, 1984

Zusman J: Quality assurance in mental health care. Hosp Community Psychiatry 39:1286–1290, 1988

Zwelling SS: Quest for a Cure: The Public Hospital in Williamsburg, 1773–1885. Williamsburg, VA, Colonial Williamsburg Foundation, 1985

Index

Page numbers printed in **boldface** *type refer to tables or figures.*

Tobacco, smoking cessation,
    health maintenance, 37
Token economy, importance of,
    for geriatric patients, 42
Transinstitutionalization, geriatric
    patients, 2–3
Treatment plan,
    33–34
    family caretaker, involvement
        in, 31
Trends, in patient population,
    change in, 5–9

Tricyclic antidepressants, 40

V
Vitamin intake, health
    maintenance, 37
Voluntary hospitalization,
    dementia, 55

W
Weight gain or loss, health
    maintenance, 37–38